Twayne's United States Authors Series

Sylvia E. Bowman, *Editor*

INDIANA UNIVERSITY

George Kelly

TUSAS 259

George Kelly

GEORGE KELLY

By FOSTER HIRSCH

Brooklyn College

TWAYNE PUBLISHERS

A DIVISION OF G. K. HALL & CO., BOSTON

Library of Congress Cataloging in Publication Data

Hirsch, Foster.
  George Kelly.

  (Twayne's United States authors series; TUSAS 259)
  Bibliography pp. 133–35.
  Includes index.
  1. Kelly, George Edward, 1887–1974.
PS3521.E425Z7   812'.5'2 [B]   75-2086
ISBN 0-8057-7158-1

PS
3521
.E425
27

Contents

About the Author

Preface

Acknowledgments

Chronology

1. A Life in the Theater   13

2. The Kelly Play   24

3. The Vaudeville Sketches   35

4. The Popular Plays   50

5. The Problem Plays   75

6. Two Plays about the Theater   95

7. The Kelly Matron   107

Notes and References   121

Selected Bibliography   133

Index   136

About the Author

Foster Hirsch received his B.A. degree from Stanford University (1965). His graduate degrees from Columbia University include an M.F.A. in Film (1966), and the M.A. (1967) and Ph.D. (1971) in English. From 1969–1971 he was a Lecturer on Drama at The New School. He is currently Assistant Professor of English and film at Brooklyn College.

A free-lance writer, Dr. Hirsch has published articles and reviews on literature, film and theater in numerous publications, including the *New York Times, The New Republic, The Chicago Tribune Book World, The Nation, Commonweal, America, The Village Voice, Variety, Film Quarterly, Cinema, Film Comment* and *Film Heritage.* He has written books on *Tennessee Williams, Elizabeth Taylor, Edward G. Robinson, Laurence Olivier* and *The Epic Film.*

Preface

In a wise and witty essay about George Kelly, Mary McCarthy wrote that he represents "the unique case of a writer who is a box-office success, an esoteric excitement, and a name utterly unregarded by the serious intellectual public. . . . This after-dinner sluggishness on the part of his public must explain the fact that he has been allowed to pass unremarked, for he is the queerest writer on view in America."[1] Miss McCarthy was writing at the end of Kelly's career—his direction of the 1947 revival of *Craig's Wife* was his final work in the theater—but her comments about the neglect and misrepresentation of Kelly are still apt today; for, over twenty-five years after his exit from Broadway, Kelly has still been "allowed to pass unremarked."

The following study is an attempt to correct this critical injustice and to place Kelly where he belongs—among top ranking American playwrights. Critics, always respectful of Kelly, mistakenly classified him as a Realistic writer. Although the plays certainly have Realistic foundations, to describe the Kelly Play as Realistic and to go no farther does not do the playwright justice; for the themes and character types, the distinctive Kelly dialogue and the unfailing Kelly rhythm, are too singular, too much of the theater, to be made to fit comfortably into a Realistic tradition. Altogether distinctive, the Kelly Play belongs to no clear-cut tradition in American letters. My purpose is, therefore, to define the peculiar pleasures and the specialized ingredients of the Kelly Play.

Even when the critics did not understand or appreciate what Kelly was trying to do, they had high regard for him and his work. In the 1920's, during the height of his fame, Kelly was considered a superior box-office dramatist as the author of three successive Broadway hits: *The Torch-Bearers*, *The Show-Off*, and *Craig's Wife* (which won the Pulitzer Prize). But Kelly disliked the designation of commercial playwright, and the seven plays that followed *Craig's Wife* were written to dispel the unwanted reputation of being merely an entertaining writer. Even in his conspicuously audience-pleasing plays, Kelly regarded himself as a moralist; for he wrote plays in order to enforce his convictions about universal human shortcomings. Kelly consciously thought of himself as a message playwright—and part of what distinguishes his work from everyone else's are the special kinds of messages he chose to deliver.

Kelly's career falls conveniently into various phases, and I have chosen these distinct periods for my chapter divisions. Chapter 1, which serves as general introduction, includes accounts of Kelly's family history, his early experiences as an actor in touring companies, and his work in vaudeville as actor-director-playwright. Chapter 2, which offers an introduction to the world of the Kelly Play, concerns themes, settings, structure, characters, tone, and rhythm of the typical play and also Kelly's own ideas about the purpose of theater as well as his theories of writing and directing. Kelly's earliest writing consisted of vaudeville sketches, and these are the subject of Chapter 3; the sketches are particularly significant because they anticipate both the manner and the matter of Kelly's ten full-length plays. Kelly's first three plays for the "legitimate" theater (Chapter 4) were his greatest critical and his only financial successes; his following three plays (Chapter 5) were decidedly less popular in conception—they represent Kelly moving into more personal themes, and they are works of more purely private focus than the popular plays. Kelly wrote only four plays during the 1930's and 1940's, and these form two distinct groupings: his two 1930's plays (Chapter 6) are theater stories, and they are more conventional in structure and general treatment than the rest of Kelly's work. But his two final plays (Chapter 7) are among his most eccentric and delightful creations; and they focus on his favorite character type, the suburban matron.

This book, the first full-length study of Kelly's plays, is designed, then, to rescue a special American playwright from the relative obscurity to which he has been unfairly consigned; to establish Kelly's high and individual place in American drama; and, most importantly, to encourage students and lovers of drama to read the work of a most unusual, most rewarding, and most colorful playwright.

Brooklyn College   FOSTER HIRSCH

Acknowledgments

George Kelly and Samuel French, Inc., for permission to quote from Kelly's plays; *The New Republic, The Nation,* and *Commonweal*, for permission to quote from the reviews of Stark Young, Joseph Wood Krutch, and Kappo Phelan; the staff of The Theater Collection of the New York Public Library at Lincoln Center; the staff of the Theater Collection at The Museum of the City of New York; the Players Club.

Chronology

1887   George Kelly born in Schuykill Falls, Pennsylvania.
1911– Played leading role in national touring company of
1912   *The Virginian*.
1913   Played in national touring company of *Live Wires*.
1914   Played in national touring company of *The Common Law*.
1915   Entered vaudeville. Acted in Paul Armstrong's *Woman Proposes*.
1916   Wrote, acted in, and directed *Finders Keepers* for the Keith-Orpheum vaudeville circuit.
1917   Joined the army for one year.
1918– Wrote, directed, toured with a dozen of his own vaudeville
1922   sketches, including *The Flattering Word, Poor Aubrey, The Weak Spot, Smarty's Party, Mrs. Ritter Appears, Mrs. Wellington's Surprise, One of Those Things*.
1922   *The Torch-Bearers* produced on Broadway.
1924   *The Show-Off* produced on Broadway.
1925   *Craig's Wife* produced on Broadway. Won Pulitzer Prize.
1926   *Daisy Mayme* produced on Broadway.
1927   *A La Carte* produced on Broadway. *Behold the Bridegroom* produced on Broadway.
1929   *Maggie the Magnificent* produced on Broadway.
1931   *Philip Goes Forth* produced on Broadway.
1935   Wrote film script for *Old Hutch*.
1936   *Reflected Glory* produced in California and on Broadway.
1938   Directed West Coast revival of *The Torch-Bearers*.
1945   *The Deep Mrs. Sykes* produced on Broadway.
1946   *The Fatal Weakness* produced on Broadway.
1947   Directed Broadway revival of *Craig's Wife*.
1956   Wrote teleplay for Shirley Booth about Perle Mesta.
1967   *The Show-Off* revived on Broadway and followed by national tour.
1974   Died, June 18, 1974, Bryn Mawr, Pennsylvania.

CHAPTER 1

A Life in the Theater

IN the first act of *The Torch-Bearers*, George Kelly's first full-length play, Mrs. Ritter asks her maid to bring a glass of water for a thirsty guest. A minute or two later, while Mrs. Ritter and her friend are busy discussing plans for their amateur theatrical, the maid enters, ceremoniously bearing a glass of water on a silver tray. In the first act of *The Fatal Weakness*, George Kelly's last produced play, Mrs. Espenshade asks *her* maid to bring in a glass of water to refresh her thirsty and loquacious friend, Mrs. Mabel Wentz. Again, while the ladies are busily engaged in plotting a scheme to determine whether or not Mr. Espenshade is having an affair with a lady doctor, the maid enters—bearing the glass of water on the silver tray.

Unlike the use of props in the well-made plays of nineteenth-century French dramatist Eugene Scribe, Kelly's glass of water does not have an integral connection to the working out of his plots; the glass of water is merely a digression, a piece of business that confers on the plays a sense both of realistic detailing and of stylistic heightening: people in real life do, after all, drink glasses of water when they are thirsty. But most people do not treat the event with such ritualistic dignity and such elaborate paraphernalia as maids, silver trays, and chit-chat about who wants or does not want a glass of water, and why she wants or does not want it.

These interludes with glasses of water are archetypal moments in the Kelly Play: to appreciate their particular use and significance is to begin to understand the playwright's special, indeed singular, world. Life as it is lived on the Kelly stage is not quite the same as it is anywhere else. The Kelly glass of water—not there for purposes of plot or characterization—is a piece of theater business, plain and simple. It's there for rhythm; the introduction of the glass of water adds a grace note to the play's movement and it establishes as well the rhythm of a character since the actor punctuates his speeches with precisely timed sips from the ceremonial glass. The glass of water is a sophisticated variation on the telephone—except that playwrights who use the telephone *need* the telephone, whereas Kelly brings in that glass of water for theatrical decoration. Rhythm, timing, the use of props, concern with material objects, small talk, social politeness (choruses of "please" and "thank you")—the glass of water is a summons for these staples of the Kelly Play. That seemingly innocent prop testifies to Kelly's status as a true man of the theater, for only a playwright who is also an actor and a director and who has had extensive practical experience in theater could possibly give so much prominence to such "business."

The biographical information on Kelly (what little there is) notes that he was "privately educated"; but, whatever his formal education may have been, there is no question that his *real* education occurred in the theater. Kelly made his debut as an actor in 1911; in 1915, he began appearing in vaudeville sketches of his own; when, in 1922, he wrote and directed *The Torch-Bearers*, the principal influence on his work was his ten years of experience "on the road." Actor, director, playwright, Kelly was indeed a man of the theater. Neither scholar nor intellectual, Kelly had but scant acquaintance with dramatic literature at the time he was writing. He was more familiar with Clyde Fitch than with Henrik Ibsen, August Strindberg, or Anton Chekhov, though his plays have been more often compared to the masters' than to Fitch's. Kelly was a *practical* man of the theater whose particular gifts—his uncanny ability for mimicry, his remarkable feel for rhythmical dialogue that is both lifelike and subtly stylized, and his instinct for what will "hold" on the stage—are quintessentially theatrical.

I *A Private Life*

George Kelly was born in Schuykill Falls, Pennsylvania, in 1887. Aside from bits and pieces such as the vague reference to his "private" education, Kelly's personal life was uncharted territory—which was exactly the way Kelly always wanted it. During his heyday, Kelly was willing to give press interviews; but he never allowed personal questions, just as he did not mind "what kind of laying out he got from the critics so long as there was no mention of personality."[1] The Kelly biography, then, is almost exclusively a matter of public record: the man (or as much of him as we have any right to know) is revealed through his work. Even at the height of his fame in the 1920's, Kelly was reclusive, "the most inward of men,"[2] with something of the reputation of a hermit. He always had "very few friends, and he [chose] them with greatest care."[3] Kelly always believed that "playwriting must be impersonal,"[4] but his idiosyncratic plays, which suggest their author's particular likes and dislikes, are in fact highly personal.

In 1911 Kelly began to act, touring in popular successes such as *The Virginian;* in 1914 he entered vaudeville, appearing in a sketch by Paul Armstrong called *Woman Proposes;* in 1915 he appeared in vaudeville in a sketch of his own, *Finders Keepers;* in 1917, his vaudeville career was interrupted by a year in the army; in 1922 Kelly left vaudeville to go "legit." From *The Torch-Bearers* in 1922 to *The Fatal Weakness* in 1945, Kelly wrote ten full-length plays; he won the Pulitzer Prize in 1925 for *Craig's Wife*, but missed the award by a margin the year before for *The Show-Off*.

Disgruntled by the commercial failure of his plays from *Daisy Mayme* in 1926 to *Philip Goes Forth* in 1931, Kelly decided to leave New York; and he left for Hollywood in 1931 to work as a screenwriter and as a script consultant. He returned to the theater in 1936 with *Reflected Glory*, and he closed his career in the 1940's with a flurry of activity: the production of *The Deep Mrs. Sykes* (1945) and *The Fatal Weakness* (1945–46) and the direction of the 1947 revival of *Criag's Wife*. After that, he wrote four plays that have neither been published nor produced: "Where the Heart Is"; "When All Else Fails," which was announced for production in 1951; a tragedy, "Can Two Walk Together?"; and "Rude Awakening." In 1956, Kelly wrote a teleplay about Perle Mesta for Shirley Booth. From 1957 until his death in June, 1974, Kelly, a life-long bachelor, lived in Southern California ("for the weather") in a retirement community which, he says, sounding like many of the characters in his plays, has "none of the gossipy quality of small towns."[5]

There are obvious gaps in the record, particularly from 1931 to 1936, from 1937 to 1944, and from 1948 to 1974. These intervals mark interruptions in the public record when Kelly was traveling (a particular hobby), script-consulting in Hollywood, being prevented from working by periods of illness, or, as Kelly said, "just coasting."

II *The Kelly Family*

George Kelly came from the famous Philadelphia Kellys—a re-markable family. His older brother Walter was an internationally popular vaudeville monologuist. His brother John Kelly, the Olym-pic rowing champion, was "the only American to win the Olympic Games single sculls, and the only one in the world to win the single and doubles in the same Olympics."[6] John Kelly was also the Chairman of the Democratic City Commission of Philadelphia and the State Secretary of Revenue, but his most famous role was that of father to Princess Grace of Monaco. Indeed, until his death, George Kelly was mentioned occasionally in the press as Princess Grace's Pulitzer Prize-winning uncle.

With two other brothers, John Kelly started a prosperous con-struction firm: "The Kellys have long been about as conspicuous as Philadelphia's 30th Street Pennsylvania Station, which, like about seventy-five per cent of the city's important office buildings, bears the credit: Brickwork by Kelly."[7] It is peculiarly fitting that George Kelly came from a family that has prospered with a construction business, for his own plays are often about houses, and his charac-ters' principal desire is often to own a house. Before he left for the stage, Kelly worked briefly as a draftsman, thereby contributing to the Kelly "construction": "Many of the bridges now standing in Chile weren't erected until the plans were marked: 'O.K. GK.' "[8]

An old, solid, venerable American family, these Philadelphia Kel-lys offer a suitable subject for a very right-wing, very sentimen-talized biography by sports enthusiast John McCallum: "Deep in our hearts we know that the present security and the future of our nation always have hinged on The Great American Family; families like that of the Philadelphia Kellys. . . . They are an energetic, rugged and unyielding lineage, slaves to their own strict stan-dards."[9] Scoop Conlon's introduction to the biography has the same worshipful tone: "an ideal American family . . . they represent what we admire in people—high principles as well as ambitions, modesty and sportsmanship as well as courage and determination to excel; clean living; religious people of tolerance, humor and de-cency. The Kellys are truly all-Americans."[10]

Always frail because of weak health, Kelly, who never went to a baseball or football game in his life, certainly did not share the Kelly mania for sports—did not seem, in fact, to fit very snugly into this

John Wayne kind of American family. But the deep-rooted Puritanism of the family heritage *does* get into the plays—the sober, religious, strait-laced Kelly family background had an unmistakable impact on Kelly the playwright. Though direct references to religion are lacking in the plays, Kelly's orthodox Irish Catholic background can be felt as a continual undercurrent; indeed, Kelly always regarded his comedies, as well as the more straight-faced works, as "pledged to a spirtual duty."[11]

Interviewers often found in Kelly a "mystic quality," as Montrose Moses has observed: "Let me suggest to anyone who contemplates interviewing Mr. Kelly . . . that he read his Bible . . . that he take down his Emerson and peruse most carefully such essays as The Over-Soul and Compensation; that he commune for a while with the writings of the Saints . . . there will flow . . . sayings from Saint Paul and whole chapters from the Gospels. They come from his fingertips, they thrill him, they are the living principle which moves him. There is spirtual exaltation in the man."[12]

Despite the "meanness" of Kelly's subjects—the unexalted middle-class homes, the follies of suburbia—the plays suggest the family-inspired Puritanical consciousness of their author. Even in his most popular plays, Kelly wrote to enforce a moral point; and Kelly's first allegiance was always to his personal morality which led him to attack the kinds of people who offended it and to support those few who did not. Such moral fastidiousness is doubtless traceable to the staunch and respectable Kelly family.

III   *Kelly the Actor*

Kelly's first interest in the theater was in acting; indeed, when he started out, he had no idea that he would eventually become a writer. He began to write in the first place only in order to provide himself a good sketch for his vaudeville act; and his first one-act play, *Finders Keepers*, was tailor-made for his own talents and personality. From 1911 to 1916, Kelly played in touring companies of popular plays. The plays, and the roles he played in them, were very different from what his own work was to be. He toured extensively in three potboilers: *The Virginian* (1911–12); *Live Wires* (1913); and *The Common Law* (1914). Adapted by Kirk LaShelle from Owen Wister's novel, *The Virginian* was the sort of Western spectacular that the movies were to claim as their own. Kelly played the hero, "an illiterate, big-souled cowpuncher,"[13] who wins a refined Eastern schoolteacher after many setbacks and discouragements.

It is hard to envision Kelly in the role of a cowboy, a rough-and-ready character who has "killed his man; gambled; not lived a life of spotless purity; helps to lynch some cattle thieves"; but who is, withal, "strong, brave, generous, sound at heart"—"a man who is a man."[14] The early roles he wrote for himself in vaudeville, the morally fastidious husband in *Finders Keepers* and the sartorial actor in *The Flattering Word*, indicate that Kelly himself had quite different concepts of his abilities. Indeed, the role of the Puritanical, civilizing schoolteacher, *The Virginian*'s heroine, is closer to the Kelly persona than the unpolished hero. Moreover, the action, the celebration of masculine strength and womanly virtue, and the exaltation of the transforming power of romance of *The Virginian* are worlds removed from Kelly's unromantic plays in which women too often try to usurp the position of "masculine strength" and men are too often full of "womanly virtue" for their own good.

Kelly's next assignment, in *Live Wires*, was equally foreign to his temperament, just as the vehicle itself contradicted his idea of what a play should be. *Live Wires* "tells the story of how a pretty telephone girl is won by a young fellow who sacrifices himself for the time being to save her brother, who has assaulted a police officer."[15] Improbably, Kelly played this sacrificing hero in a "sketch [that] is full of comedy and pathos and [that] never fails to win merited applause."[16]

A dramatization of "the most sensational novel of the century," *The Common Law* was more in line with Kelly's subsequent development as an actor and as a playwright. In this drama, Kelly played an artist who wants to marry a model who is an "advanced thinker," and who denounces the concept of marriage. The artist (and here Kelly had a role that suited his didactic penchant) tries to convince her that "to live with him without the marriage ceremony being performed would expose her to scandal and gossip. . . . It is only after they have been socially ostracized that the girl realizes the error of her belief and consents to abide by the decree of law and convention."[17] The moral "education" of an errant female is a recurrent Kelly motif. In his own work, however, Kelly is never so melodramatic as *The Common Law* is; and, while his morality may be as conservative and as old-fashioned, it never seems so tritely provincial as it does in this play.

Though Kelly was cast against his type in two of these plays, he always received favorable reviews; and he was particularly praised for the naturalness of his acting and for the originality of his interpretations. When his favorable notices won the attention of Paul Armstrong, who was looking for a male lead for his one-act play, *Woman Proposes*, to be performed on the vaudeville circuit, Kelly got the part; and his success in it made him a vaudeville headliner. Kelly's subsequent frustrating search for material that would provide him a worthy successor to the Armstrong play led to his writing his own vehicle.

IV *Walter Kelly*

When Tony Pastor opened his famous theater on October 24, 1881, he inaugurated a new era in vaudeville: "a straight clean variety show, the first—as such—ever given in this country."[18] By the time Kelly entered vaudeville in 1915, it was a respected *family* entertainment and was not synonymous with "girly" shows and smutty comedians. It was professional, it had "class," and "Kelly could say, with just pride, that he was a headliner during that time when Nazimova and Madame Bernhardt were being featured as vaudevillians."[19]

Kelly's own "clean" sketches, of course, gave added "tone" to vaudeville; and his one-acts were part of a vaudeville tradition begun in 1893—"legit" stars in sketch acts. The first such sketch, written by an actress named Francesca Redding, was called *A Happy Pair*. In a lively history of vaudeville, Douglas Gilbert writes that "its thirty-minute act told a clean domestic story in which no singing, dancing, gagging, or topical allusions occurred. A novelty? It was a feat."[20]

It was, then, no disgrace for a member of the respectable Kelly family to go into vaudeville. At the time, in fact, Philadelphia had the reputation of being "the cradle of vaudeville";[21] and when the new Keith house opened, the producers "laid out the royal carpet for a Main Line audience and the theater opened with the decorum of the Metropolitan Opera. Some of the city's snootiest families subscribed for weekly locations."[22] Moreover, when George entered vaudeville, he was only following family precedent: his older brother Walter was firmly established as a monologuist.[23] Their personalities and their material were quite different, but the Kelly brothers shared the gift of mimicry. They were both "students of types," particularly *American* types: "George could hear a conversation, come home and repeat everything that had been said, just the way it had been said. . . . George and Walter had one big thing in common: They had only to look out and study real life to find their fortunes."[24]

Walter Kelly made *his* fortune by telling stories about Southern blacks who appear before "The Virginia Judge," a role he played in vaudeville for over thirty years. The Judge was based on a character drawn from life, "Judge Brown, a philospher and wit, a tall, gaunt Virginian . . . before whom dozens of Negro miscreants paraded daily."[25] Walter Kelly was universally recognized as "the best raconteur of darkey stories on the stage."[26] Though best known for his Southern dialects, Walter Kelly was also proficient in cockney, Scottish, Irish, Jewish, Italian, and New England Yankee dialects.[27]

Kelly was popular everywhere: in the South as well as in the North, and in such far-flung places as Egypt, Australia, South Africa, Ireland, and Wales. Like Will Rogers (to whom he was often compared for his humanism and his droll wit), Walter Kelly was an international favorite. And, unlike his saturnine playwright-brother, Walter was a bon vivant. Heavy set, jovial, and a great sports fan and good friend to most of the prominent sports figures of the time, Walter led a jolly, turn-of-the-century kind of life.[28]

George Kelly felt that the vaudeville of his and his brother's day is altogether misunderstood by "the younger generation": "Walter was a man of dignity and good taste," he said, "certainly not a burlesque comedian."[29] But surely this younger generation would find it hard to laugh at Walter Kelly's characterization of the black man as the wily, shiftless, no-account Uncle Tom of these typical Virginia Judge anecdotes:

"Judge," said the Negro, "I want to plead not guilty. I didn't want to cut nobody. I just sorta pushed the oyster knife to'd him and he just sorta ran into it."

"Jim," the judge said, "this is a serious case. Have you a lawyer?"

"No, suh," the prisoner replied. "I don't wants no lawyer, but if you don't mind I certainly would like a couple of witnesses."[30]

The first up before the bar of justice is Flatiron. So she's like to have her worthless man arrested this a-coming Thursday. Why Thursday? Why, because the doctor he says he ought to be out of the hospital by that time.[31]

Kelly's stories, with their paternalistic condescension and their careful dialectal distinctions between "the nigger and the southern gentleman,"[32] would not be readily accepted by contemporary audiences. Moreover, Walter Kelly's refusal in 1909 to appear on the same stage with a black song-and-dance team, Williams and Walker, would be no credit to him today. Even in 1909 the reaction of Walker was that "The man is foolish. The day is past for that sort of thing. Both white men and black have a right to earn a living in whatever manner they find most congenial, provided they injure no one else in so doing." Douglas Gilbert, who records Walker's remark, adds that "There is no record of Kelly's rejoinder."[33]

George shared with his older brother ideas that today seem old-fashioned and undemocratic; for, like Walter, George assumed the division of society into classes. As the characters and the action of play after play suggest, he accepted as social fact the distinction between masters and servants. Just as in Walter Kelly's comic world there are white judges to evaluate black miscreants, so in George Kelly's plays there are upper-middle-class matrons to order servants to bring in glasses of water on silver trays. Neither Walter nor George questioned for a moment the propriety of "class."

Like George, Walter never married; and some of his public statements indicate (like many of George's plays) a decided misogynistic strain in the male-oriented Kelly family that accepted as gospel "a man's a man" and "a woman's a woman." In an angry moment in his autobiography *Of Me I Sing*, Walter wrote: " . . . it is an undoubted fact that America is now closer to being an absolute matriarchy than any nation in recorded history. . . . [women] hold the power of life and death over any motion picture, play, book, magazine, or newspaper. They have demanded and received absolute equality in every field of activity, with one exception—they still permit the Boy Friend to pay the dinner check."[34]

The brothers were again alike in complaining of the decay of vaudeville in regard to morality and the standard of professionalism. Walter many times decried the "postwar letdown in stage morals . . . this theatrical debauch percolated into the movie palaces,

which seemed to be trying to outdo the speaking stage in filth."[35] Walter Kelly maintained that "more than fifty percent" of the audience that went to see "filth" were "the female of the species. For proof of this statement, one has only to note the patrons who mob each other at court trials of the most ghastly murders of sex-crimes and gloat over evidence which would drive a normal mind to a washroom."[36]

Around 1920, George, too, began to speak freely to the press, offering his conviction that vaudeville had begun to "deteriorate." Newspapers carried a particularly significant incident in which Kelly was involved. While on tour, Kelly complained to the managers that a performer named Ails had used "objectionable language in the presence of a female member of his act." Kelly announced that such behavior was symptomatic of the decline of vaudeville and that he would cancel all future bookings on the same bill with Ails.[37]

Brilliant mimics, shrewd observers of types, both droll Kelly brothers were clearly influenced by the conservative moral, social, and religious tradition of the large Kelly family. Both were conservative if not downright reactionary in their class-conscious view of society, in their absolute distinctions between male and female, and in their dislike of racy language and sexy entertainment. Both were American Puritans.

IV *Kelly in Hollywood*

Like his brother Walter, George Kelly scorned the movies; for both Kellys believed that the theater was the highest and most respectable form of entertainment. George never owned a television, and he rarely went to see films. But in 1931, when he was disgusted with Broadway, he was persuaded by a friend to go to Hollywood. Since he hated cold weather, Kelly was lured to California as much as anything by the promise of a warm and sunny climate. When he left New York in 1931, he said that he was "going to the coast with no preconceived ideas, either favorable or unfavorable, about motion pictures. I know nothing about them right now, and I want to spend several weeks studying how they're made. Then I can decide whether I like the work or not."[38] It didn't take him long to decide that, in fact, he didn't like the work: "If you realize from the start that you can't work alone and creatively in the same way you do with a play, you're safe."[39] But Kelly didn't want to be "safe"; and, with the royalties he was collecting, he certainly didn't need to be.

He worked, however, as script consultant for several films at Metro-Goldwyn-Mayer, but "they weren't anything he wanted to put his name to."[40] The only screen credit he received was for his work on the script of a 1935 film, *Old Hutch*, in which the dominant personality was not Kelly's but that of the film's star, Wallace Beery. Based on a story by Garrett Smith, "Old Hutch Lives Up To It," which appeared in *The Saturday Evening Post* of February 28, 1920, the movie is about a lazy rustic who finds a hundred thousand dollars, hides it, and goes to work to pretend he has some money, only to have the gangsters whose money it is steal it from him; when he captures them, he enjoys the reward money and becomes a reformed character and responsible member of the community.

The film's incipient moral lesson is Kelly-like, and the rustic dialect affords him an opportunity to write his homespun dialogue; but the general sentimentality of the film, the innocuous secondary lovers, and the folksy charm of it all are not the usual marks of Kelly's work. The film's non-Kelly features testify to a method of working in which the writer, "after every 25 pages, would bring the script into conference, and they would tell me what to do from that point on."[41] For a playwright who insisted on directing each of his plays, who cast each role, and who had complete and final say in each aspect of production, the films' collaborative procedure was naturally uncongenial. Kelly's fate was similar to that of other established writers imported to Hollywood in the 1930's in that the particular flavor of his writing—the reason he was hired in the first place—was never translated intact to the screen.[42]

CHAPTER 2

The Kelly Play

KELLY has been compared with Ibsen, Strindberg, and Chekhov; with Sir Arthur Wing Pinero and Henry Arthur Jones; with Clyde Fitch; with Henry James; and with his contemporaries Philip Barry, George Abbott, George S. Kaufman and Moss Hart, Sidney Howard, and S. N. Behrman. Though Kelly's plays sometimes resemble the work of each of these writers, there are no direct or close influences. Kelly several times expressed his admiration for Ibsen and Strindberg, but at the time he wrote his most Ibsen-like play, *Craig's Wife*, he was barely familiar with Ibsen's work.[1] As early as Kelly's vaudeville one-act *Finders Keepers*, reviewers noted Strindbergian underpinnings—though all they meant was that Kelly's husband and wife, like most of Strindberg's, acted out elemental hostilities. It wasn't until much later—*after* his major period in the 1920's—that Kelly did the bulk of his reading in dramatic literature.

Among the writers with whom he has most often been compared, Kelly was most familiar with Clyde Fitch, the prolific popular entertainer whose plays—melodramatic and nineteenth-century as they now seem—nonetheless comprise the most respectable collection of any pre-Eugene O'Neill American dramatist. In his time, Fitch was considered an acute character portraitist; but, though his *Girl With Green Eyes* is a study of an aspect, or quirk, of female psychology, Fitch's and Kelly's plays about women belong to two separate eras. Fitch's artificial melodrama is clearly the residue of an ignoble pot-boiler tradition, while Kelly's female portraits are more firmly in the tradition of "modern drama."

I *An Instinctive Playwright*

In both writing and production, the Golden Age for American drama was the 1920's. Moving restlessly between realistic character studies and Continental expressionism, Eugene O'Neill was the great experimenter of the period, the author who set the pace. In his shadow, writers like Barry, Behrman, Howard, Elmer Rice, Kaufman, Maxwell Anderson, and Kelly began to look at American life and manners more closely than earlier dramatists had. For the first time in American drama, plays had solidity and polish; and they could qualify as literature rather than as ephemeral entertainment. The revolutions in form and content that had marked European theater since Ibsen's problem plays in the 1880's had at last begun to be reflected in American drama; and, as a result, complex, rounded characters began to replace the stock cardboard figures that had dominated American plays.

The Provincetown Playhouse, the Theater Guild, and Eva Le Gallienne's Civic Repertory Theater were formed to encourage the production of ambitious though not necessarily commercial native plays as well as difficult and influential foreign ones. And, for the first time in American theater history, serious, talented writers had the opportunity to get their work before an audience. The playwrights whom we still consider worth reading occupied only a small fraction of the Broadway offerings, however. In 1929, at the end of the decade, Kelly's *Maggie the Magnificent* competed for the attention of Broadway audiences with theatrical fare that was clearly popular—star-dominated rather than playwright-oriented: Eddie Cantor in *Whoopee;* Mrs. Fisk in *Ladies of the Jury;* George M. Cohan in *Gambling;* Otis Skinner in *A Hundred Years Old;* Gertrude Lawrence in *Candle-Light;* and revues such as *Hot Chocolate* and *George White's Scandals*. Eva Le Gallienne was continuing to offer the most ambitious and intelligent theater in town at the Civic Repertory Theater on 14th Street. Apart from Kelly's play, the only other "author" play was *Strictly Dishonorable* by a young man named Preston Sturges who later distinguished himself as one of the most original writer-directors of comedy—in films.

Kelly was part of this colorful theatrical decade which was a mixture of the staple low-brow entertainment and the first sustained attempts of American dramatists to reach for higher levels of invention. But the playwrights who got started in the 1920's, and who contributed significantly to American drama for several decades afterwards, were not in any sense a group; and Kelly was less a part of any group than the others. Reclusive, an inveterate non-party-goer, Kelly simply did his own work. Though the drawing-room tone of some of his work suggests comparison with Barry and Behrman, those chroniclers of our upper classes, and though *Craig's Wife* in its character-drawing of a rapacious and castrating female has similarities to Howard's malignant mother in *The Silver Cord*, Kelly's work has internal rather than external cross-references.

"No one ever taught me anything about writing, acting, or directing," Kelly asserted. "I just knew it. Either you have the ability or you don't. I don't know how to write any other way."[2] Kelly was a great original and, in a way, a great primitive. No one ever had to tell him anything; with his intuitive sense of theater, he merely needed experience to test and to perfect his innate ability. The real, perhaps the only, influence on Kelly's writing was his own experience in the theater as an actor in touring companies of pulp-like popular successes and as an actor-director-playwright for the two-a-day. As Carl Carmer has observed, "While Philip Barry was learning theory under professors of the drama, George Kelly was practicing in the two-a-day. . . . If one knew no other fact than this about them it would not be a difficult matter correctly to identify each as the author of his own work."[3] In *Philip Goes Forth*, Kelly takes a swipe at playwrights who learn their craft at school, and at professors (did Kelly have in mind George Pierce Baker?) who reduce drama to textbook theory.

II   *Something about the Weather*

Lighting a cigarette; drinking a glass of water or a cup of coffee, punctuating speeches with meticulously timed sips; folding a newspaper; darning socks; small talk or chit-chat, about the weather or what the neighbors are doing, have done, or will do; disquisitions on dinner menus and on determining the precise time; giving and receiving detailed information about addresses—such activity provides not merely the warm-up to, but the basic substance of, the Kelly Play. Mary McCarthy beautifully captures the eccentric and lopsided angle of repose of Kelly's dances of objects:

Their complete cast of characters is not listed on the program, the real heroes and heroines being glasses of water, pocketbooks, telephones, and after-dinner coffee cups. It is difficult to describe a George Kelly play to anyone who has not seen several, simply because it is not like anything else while on the surface it resembles every play one has ever been to . . . It takes a second or third George Kelly play for the spectator to perceive, with the horror he remembers from dreams, that the stage business is every-

thing. . . . The George Kelly play . . . is a long ad-lib. Its subject is in-
anity. Stage-time here, like life-time, is an interminable gap which must
be bridged by desperate conversational maneuvers, remarks about the
weather, the time of day, vital statistics, golf scores, menus, clothes, train
schedules, people's addresses. . . . This gabble is the chorus which speaks
the meaning of the play; and like a chorus it has its pantomimic expression
in a compulsive dance of pocketbooks, pencils, fancy work, glasses of water,
hats, timetables, and newspapers. The pocketbook is the leader of the
chorus. . . . the heroine's pocketbook is always resting on a lower shelf of
the audience's mind.[4]

Kelly himself did not know how to classify his writing, except that
it is "realistic. Writing should be a reflection of life."[5] Compilers of
drama anthologies and historians of American drama have taken
Kelly at his word, and he is invariably labeled as an "early American
realist." Kelly's plays certainly reflect the surfaces of life, but it is
precisely their obsessive concern with surfaces, with the minute
business of daily living, which gives the plays such a peculiar slant,
and which makes "Realism" an inadequate description for the mode
of the plays. Kelly's most famous play, *The Show-Off*, can be safely
described as a work of American Realism, but the designation will
not quite do for any other Kelly play. Kelly may well believe that his
plays reflect life directly, whereas life as it is lived in his plays—that
"compulsive dance" of pocketbooks and buttons and timetables—is
"Realism" filtered through the lens of a special imagination.

This Realism is of a peculiarly heightened, selective, and rarefied
kind in the same way that Kelly's dialogue, with its overlapping
speeches, its pauses and stumblings and repetitions, its dying falls
and trailing sentences, its persistent patter of "Well, but . . . " has a
surface verisimilitude—seems at times a transcription from life. The
rhythm of the dialogue is, however, too neat, too entirely successful, and too beautifully coordinated to pass for untampered reality
(or even Realism). A more accurate description of Kelly's work
might be "Theatricality superimposed upon a precise realism."[6]

III   *The Production*

The passion for precision that animates Kelly's characters ("I was
visiting my relatives out in Milwaukee," says the deep Mrs. Sykes.
"Milwaukee, Wisconsin, you mean?" asks her friend, a character
who could have been created only by Kelly) was likewise a distinguishing trait of the Kelly production. And the Kelly production,

superintended by the playwright himself down to the placement of ash trays and vases of roses, was as distinctly flavored as the plays. In the printed versions of his plays, Kelly is delightfully precise about what his characters wear (the color schemes of their wardrobes, the number of beads in their necklaces, the width of their bracelets) and about the sets—the living room floor at Mrs. Sykes', for instance, is twelve inches below the foyer. Kelly specifies the exact positioning of the omnipresent vases of roses and of the inevitably "matching" table and chairs; he describes the paintings that adorn the walls and the books that grace the bookshelves. In short, interior decoration is as important to the playwright as it is to his characters.

Kelly the director assumed control of each of his plays in order to insure the correct interpretation of the intentions of Kelly the playwright. A press release describes his invariable directorial technique:

Kelly can always be found backstage during the early performances of a new play, watching every move made by the actors and listening very carefully to every line that is spoken. He makes careful mental note of what's what, and what's not. After the performance the company is called together and his memoranda are distributed. A line is to be transposed here; a word deleted there; a "crossing" is rearranged, and a "piece of business" is put in, or taken out. The revised way of doing it is then run over by the actors and consolidated into the next performance. Kelly's usual process is one of cutting down; it is a process of snipping and clipping . . . the boiling down continues until he is satisfied. The play is then "set." It is reported on good authority that Kelly, as a rule, takes about eight performances to "set" his play. But after the play is once "set" it is not changed again. The play is then turned over to the tender care of Archie Curtis, stage manager. It is his turn now to see that all is well and kept well. He permits no deviation from the picture that Kelly has drawn and insists that each and every performance shall be identical. Liberties with word or line are anathema. A misplaced comma is promptly detected by the vigilant Archie, and the player guilty of any stage lapses or sins is handed a small slip of paper upon which is written a polite but succinct reminder of his shortcomings.[7]

As director, then, Kelly worked tirelessly, meticulously, to serve his work as an author. He felt that the playwright should direct his own work—and nobody else's: "It is hard enough to direct your own work in the theatre, without attempting to stage another writer's. I do not believe it is possible to achieve a sufficient oneness with

another's mind to give his play what it deserves. This is why I have
steadily refused numerous invitations to direct. . . . I have too
much humility to think myself possessed of sufficient wisdom to
understand another's mind and purpose."[8]

Kelly had a legendary reputation for precision and discipline. His
Mrs. Sykes, Catherine Willard, praised his methods: "In most companies I have been with the players telephone, talk to each other,
play gin-rummy or rest between scenes that they happen to be in.
But with Mr. Kelly directing, no one leaves the stage."[9] Kelly's
theories on directing, like his theories on playwriting, were simple,
intuitive, tested by experience: "The eternal verities of directing . . . are width, height, and depth. The width refers to the position of the actor on the stage when he speaks a line—whether he
moves forward, stands still, etc. The height has to do with the pitch
of the voice, the inflection. And the depth refers to the emotional
demands of the role . . . rhythm, flow, timing, 'business.'"[10]

Kelly directorial method violated the orthodox rule that the director must not play the role for the actor; instead, he must lead the
actor to discover, and thus to play, the role for himself. Kelly himself performed each actor's part. He knew exactly how he wanted
the parts played, and he allowed no room for the actor's personal or
idiosyncratic contribution to the role. Lee Tracy, who played in *The
Show-Off*, recalls: "We used to beg her [Helen Lowell, who played
Mrs. Fisher in *The Show-Off*] during rehearsals to make mistakes in
her lines, so Kelly would get up and show her how it ought to be
done. We loved to watch him. He acted the whole part right out for
her."[11] And Chrystal Herne, who played Mrs. Craig and who received much praise for her performance, was always conscious of
the fact that there was a better Mrs. Craig watching the show from
the wings.

In Kelly's directing, then, as in his writing, "nothing is left to
chance. Every inflection, every pause is carefully shaded or timed.
Positions, gestures, the disposition of the least stage property are all
specified. . . . Not so much as the turn of a hand is left to blind
chance, so precisely is every means directed and every effect calculated."[12] Kelly told Helen Lowell that, when she was seated in a
rocking chair, she was to laugh after she had rocked three times: "he
had figured that that was the second when the laugh was due.
During the early run of the play, Miss Lowell complained to him
one evening that the laugh had not gone well with the audience.

'That was because you rocked only twice before you laughed.' "[13]

Kelly was certainly rough on his actors—they were the instruments to his conductor. Yet Kelly got along with his actors; the same ones returned to work for him again and again. Mary Gildea, for instance, appeared in seven Kelly productions—always as the maid. She was emptying ash trays and dusting the matching table and chairs in 1915, and thirty-five years later she was performing the same offices. As Mary McCarthy says, "Presumably, Mr. Kelly, like his own matrons, 'would not know what to do without her.'"[14] Kelly recalled that Mary Gildea, "who had a funny little flat voice, was completely unaffected, and kept within her part," was scared to death of him; she wouldn't bat an eye without instructions from the master, wouldn't take other acting jobs unless she had his permission.[15]

Despite the rigorous pace of the Kelly rehearsal and the autocratic methods, actors liked Kelly: it was prestigious to appear in a Kelly play; he was such a perfectionist that actors were practically assured of affirmative reviews. Kelly avoided trouble with actors because he had their confidence; they knew *he* knew what he was doing: "Actors are surprisingly pliant and patient when they feel they are working with someone who is not simply a glorified stage manager. Even actors of long experience and set habits will cheerfully surrender their own style and method to enter fully into the orchestration of the scene. As soon as they are made to feel that the orchestration is the all-important thing, they are glad to accept every detail of direction and to be as exacting as I am myself."[16]

Kelly, who cast his plays himself, looked for types to play his type characters. Often, an actor's laugh or a particular movement suggested his appropriateness for a role. At the time he was looking for an actor to play the title role in *The Show-Off*, Kelly inadvertently met John Louis Bartels while he was walking in the Broadway area with his producer Rosalie Stewart. Bartels was a dancer at the time with the Follies, and he was "remarkably light" on his feet. When he greeted him with a jaunty laugh, Kelly knew at once that he had found his Aubrey Piper.[17]

Because of Kelly's fastidiousness and his vigilant writing and directing, the actor was necessarily subordinate to the over-all design of the play: Kelly was the true and ultimate *auteur* of any Kelly production. But, despite the difficulty, if not the impossibility, of doing a star turn in a play of his, Kelly worked with some of the most illustrious actresses of the American theater, all of whom were well-reviewed for their work. Josephine Hull, that delightfully befuddled comedienne, was in both *Craig's Wife* and *Daisy Mayme;* stout, droll Alison Skipworth had one of the top triumphs of her career as Mrs. J. Duro Pampinelli in *The Torch-Bearers;* Chrystal Herne had *the* top triumph of her career as Mrs. Craig; Joan Blondell got one of her biggest boosts as a result of her work as the gum-chewing flapper in *Maggie the Magnificent* (James Cagney also had a colorful part as Blondell's loutish bootlegging husband); and Judith Anderson had her first major role in America in *Behold the Bridegroom* (this was Kelly's favorite play, and Miss Anderson's was his favorite performance).

Kelly had his most challenging directing job in 1936, when he cast Tallulah Bankhead as the temperamental actress in *Reflected Glory.* They had rows at rehearsals, but they liked each other: Tallulah speaks highly of Kelly in her autobiography; Kelly said Tallulah hated acting but was a true actress nonetheless. Tallulah did manage, however, to steal the spotlight from Kelly; for, when *Reflected Glory* opened, it was Tallulah's comeback rather than Kelly's that garnered most of the public and critical interest. For the first and only time in his career, a Kelly play looked like a star vehicle, and Kelly was upstaged by a performer.

IV *The Moralist*

The Kelly Play and the Kelly Production were, therefore, synonymous with impeccable theater. Play and production were thoroughly professional; but Kelly never regarded himself merely as a polished entertainer: "I do not write for the type of person who asks you, 'What's a good show in town?' and wants only to be amused. . . . Naturally I feel there's a place for such 'good shows' but I believe in the theater of ideas. It's all right to hold a rattle before the immature, but let there also be a theater for the intelligent and the well-informed."[18] Indeed, Kelly gave statements throughout his career to the press about the "higher" purposes of theater: "In every civilized community the theater is and has always been a center of culture. It is the dwelling place of thought and inspiration no less than the church is, for the kinship of church and theater is close despite their surface antagonism. The church, where it is most effectual, is highly dramatic."[19] The similarity between church and theater is the theme of Kelly's early one-act, *The Flattering Word*.

Convinced of the potentially exalted purpose of theater, Kelly designed his plays as moral exempla; and, as Edward Maisel has recognized, "Like Roswitha the Nun composing her six plays to celebrate the virtue of chastity, George Kelly is a simple moralist using the theater for simple moral purposes."[20] Each play is written around a central moral point; and his "method of teaching the lesson is always the same. First it is embodied in a kind of rubric selected from the dialogue and prefaced to the play; then it is announced, well in advance, by one of the characters; then the protagonist earns his comeuppance or reward in conformity with it; and finally it is enunciated in enlightened retrospect."[21]

Kelly almost invariably employed as the bearer of his moral a deeply sensible, dry-eyed individual who surveys the scene from a lofty remove. Not altogether dispassionate, the Kelly *raisonneur* is nonetheless inveterately superior, self-contained, Puritanical. And his moral lessons are unfailingly simple. Through his message-bearers, Kelly offers a few homely truths as cures for the ills of mankind: "Honesty is preferable to dishonesty (*Finders Keepers*); forthrightness is better than deceit (*Smarty's Party*); modesty and humility are better than vanity (*The Torch-Bearers* and *Philip Goes Forth*); love of others and generosity oppose egoism and cupidity (*Craig's Wife* and *Daisy Mayme*); chastity in woman is not to be thrown away for weak sexual indulgences (*Behold the Bridegroom*); trust is better than mistrust or suspicion (*The Deep Mrs. Sykes*); strong passions and weak sentiments should be reason's slave (*Can Two Walk Together?* and *The Fatal Weakness*.)[22]

Kelly's moral instruction is usually related to the two basic themes of his work: vocation and the threat posed by certain kinds of overbearing women. Vocation is "the assumption of one's true post in the community, the post which determines a correct moral relation to one's fellows and to one's own inner fulfillment—that has been a continuing concern in our national life from the time of the earliest Puritans."[23] Indeed, Kelly regards the finding and the pursuit of a true vocation with almost religious awe. The theme of vocation is related particularly to theater in that those whose true vocation it is are the chosen ones; and those who are not gifted by nature for the theater must retreat from the field to save their souls and to prevent a waste of time. Kelly reserves his highest respect for the true theater artist, but he admires and establishes as a worthy example the person who does his own job well (whatever that job may be): the businessman (Philip in *Philip Goes Forth*); the social secretary (Maggie of *Maggie the Magnificent*); or the thrifty house-wife (Mrs. Fisher of *The Show-Off*).

Kelly respects those who make their own way in the world; in fact, he reserves his harshest criticism for the leeches and the para-sites (Mrs. Craig, Laura Fenner in *Daisy Mayme*, Mrs. Sykes). To do the job, to find a place in the community, to hold to the proper course—these are the anchors of Kelly's moral philosophy. And, because women, in Kelly's view, are among "the influences that hold people back, that keep them off their true course," he often criticizes them harshly.[24] The plays in which such women appear are designed as warnings to the unwary male and as deterrents to the overbearing woman. The self-justifying thief in *Finders Keepers*, the conniving flapper in *Smarty's Party*, the redoubtable Mrs. Craig, the embittered Laura Fenner, the emasculating Mrs. Sykes, are Kelly women who are "upholders and defenders of inertia."[25] They misappropriate and misuse power, steer good men off their course, and willfully mislead and destroy.

V *The Kelly Rules*

Like his morality, Kelly's prescriptions for dramatic technique can be reduced to a succinct list of "do's" and "don'ts". "Avoid vulgarity. Avoid the obvious. Don't say the thing they want you to say. Don't go too far—a laugh is good for so many beats and no more."[26] Have a clearly stated point. Know what you want to say, and don't get off the track: "Mr. Albee answered a professor friend of mine, who said his class was mystified by *Tiny Alice*, that 'It means whatever it means to you.' I think you must know what you mean or you're in the wrong medium. What would keep you glued to the typewriter for months unless you had something you wanted to say?"[27]

The play of character, Kelly feels, is the most important and meaningful kind of play—"one in which the audience can never quite catch up with what a character is going to do next. . . . The play of structure—that is, one which has everything plotted out in an easily recognizable pattern—is definitely outmoded."[28] Plot must flow from character, must be determined by character conflicts. Characters should be "universal types . . . easily recognizable, far different from the overdrawn, unreal stage creatures of the past."[29]

"Playwriting must be impersonal,"[30] Kelly insisted. "The shadow of the author must never fall across the play. . . . Whenever I see myself obtruding into my play, I change the pattern."[31] Despite his strictures against the playwright's personal intrusion into his material, Kelly's plays are inevitably personal statements. The constant struggle between the objective ideal and the subjective coloring, in fact, is one of the distinguishing features of his work.

These, then, are the signposts of that strange and delightful thing, the Kelly Play: a play of recognizable character types that enforces an elementary moral and uncovers a basic aspect of human psychology; a play curiously unlocalized, the events and characters suspended in something of a timeless vacuum; a play of private focus that assigns all ills not to society but to the individual; a play that enforces a common-sensical, conservative position, and offers advice about how to cope with life in an unromantic, clear-eyed fashion; a play that is "a dance of objects," a fantasia of the minutiae of daily life, a series of tics, ad-libs, small talk, theater business; a play that gives prominence to rhythm and gesture and movement—everything from the slightest step of each of the characters to the rhythmical pattern of the dialogue to the orchestration of the entire design of the play is coordinated with marvelous precision. The Kelly Play is rare theater, droll, meticulous, and specialized.

CHAPTER 3

The Vaudeville Sketches

I Woman Proposes

KELLY'S first appearance in vaudeville occurred after he had had five years of touring experience in the "legitimate" theater. By the time he acted in Paul Armstrong's *Woman Proposes* (1915), he was accustomed to the rigors of traveling across the country. Armstrong's "clean" sketch was a welcome change after Kelly's trouping in such uncongenial low-brow entertainment as *The Virginian* and *The Common Law*. In *Woman Proposes*, Armstrong, "whose busy fountain pen drips blood and whose fervid imagination is peopled with underworld persons of the lowest strata,"[1] had made an abrupt change and had written a satire about types of women, a subject that was to be fertile Kelly territory. Armstrong's sketch demonstrates that time and again the woman craftily manages to propose to the man. In the play, a woman approaching thirty who is anxious to avoid spinsterhood is talking to a man who is in love with her. A gullible type, he has twice before been maneuvered into marriage by designing ladies. Now, seated with the woman in "the romantic dimness of the conservatory," he tries to convince her that "woman proposes . . . they did to me and I couldn't help myself." Hidden behind an arbor, they watch as the women in three separate couples—each woman wilier, more cleverly insinuating than the other—cast, maneuver, and hook their men. The sketch ends, however, with a sentimental blurring of the satiric edge: "You see," the watching man says to his spinsterish companion, "Woman proposes, but you won't have to because I'm going to beat you to it."

Variety described the sketch as a "comedy of manners, graced with humor, scintillating with kindly satire and rounded out with a touch of sentiment," and concluded that it was decidedly "not for the lowbrows."[2] "Vinegary" satire and "subtle" psychology were not standard vaudeville fare; and *Woman Proposes*, like Kelly's work after it, represented, according to vaudeville's principal chronicler, Douglas Gilbert, "thoughtful advances from the rube-type sketches and stylized comedies which clowned up the vaudeville bills of the early 1900's. Usually the standardized sketches were developed from the hokum of mistaken identity."[3] The satiric tone of the Armstrong sketch, its subject of female wiles and the female "threat," and its sober male as the moral instructor, became staples of Kelly's own work.

II Kelly's High-Class Vaudeville

Kelly's "elevated" one-acts are preliminary drafts for material that is more fully developed in the full-length plays. One of Those Things (1918) is an initial variation on the theme of marital infidelity that Kelly returned to in The Deep Mrs. Sykes (1945) and The Fatal Weakness (1946); Smarty's Party (1922) dramatizes the opposition between "class" and vulgarity that is the concern of Maggie the Magnificent (1929); Mrs. Ritter Appears (1919), a satire on amateur theater, is a one-act version of The Torch-Bearers (1922); and Poor Aubrey (1919) is the one-act inspiration for The Show-Off (1924). The Weak Spot (1919), an exceedingly curious sketch about superstition, anticipates characteristics found in Daisy Mayme (1926) and The Deep Mrs. Sykes (1945). And the plays' settings, from the lower-middle-class suburban home in The Weak Spot to the comfortable middle-range home of the Aldrids in Finders Keepers to the smart upper-class Park Avenue drawing room in Smarty's Party are also returned to in Kelly's longer works.

Except for the farcical subject matter of Mrs. Ritter Appears, Kelly's is a singularly odd collection of vaudeville playlets. As Douglas Gilbert notes, "tragedies, psychological studies, acidulous satires set down in aloes . . . this was heady stuff for vaudeville."[4] Writing against the grain, Kelly achieved in vaudeville a degree of popularity which he attained only sporadically in his "legitimate" career: "When Kelly . . . was booked, the bills revolved around his sketches. They were not just another number . . . They were unique."[5] When he summarized Kelly's career, Joseph Wood Krutch wrote that vaudeville was "a rather odd beginning for a man whose most recent plays have been conspicuously austere."[6] But the austerity is very much evident even in the earliest sketches: Kelly always wrote to his own measure.

"I kept my integrity," Kelly said, "because in my sketches I never wrote down to the vaudeville audiences. I never made any cheap appeals to laughter or to pathos. I never compromised."[7] Kelly, proud of his career in the two-a-day, felt that, when he was in it, vaudeville was in its "golden days": "During the years I appeared the greatest players in the country were also acting in vaudeville sketches."[8] The plays had to be "top quality; the managers had to get hold of good ones because all the big stars wanted to tour in vaudeville."[9]

Though Kelly tired of vaudeville—agreeing with the popular verdict, he felt that films destroyed it—he "snort [ed] at the idea that anyone should poke fun at him for being in [it]"[10] before it degenerated into "girly shows" and farce. Kelly credited his theater sense to the training he received on the road. Educated by and in the theater, Kelly was, "more than any young American playwright of his generation, distinctly of the theater."[11] Traveling extensively, first in legitimate touring companies, and then later in his own plays, Kelly learned "to know the American audience at its most American and its most average. Kelly was his own most ruthless critic. Stop-watch in hand, he would wait for the effect he sought and if the audience's reaction was not quick enough or sure enough, out would come lines and scenes, often those he cared for most. But when the cutting was over, there was always a sketch to which an audience quickly responded. By the time he was through with vaudeville, George Kelly knew the average response to idea and emotion thoroughly."[12]

III   Finders Keepers

Kelly played in *Woman Proposes* for fifty weeks, and the success of his performance endeared him to the vaudeville managers who offered to book him for another tour if he could locate a new sketch. Kelly, who made a thorough search, could find nothing except "the usual kind of slam-bang vaudeville act," and so he decided to write a sketch of his own. The result was *Finders Keepers*, a most uncharacteristic vaudeville piece since it was much more "high-toned" for its time and place than even *Woman Proposes*. Despite its unorthodox slant, however, it proved a great hit. Ever alert to audience reaction, Kelly learned to pace his sketches with metronomic precision. "*Finders Keepers* was played straight," he said, "it was very tense. It lasted a half hour; it was not to go a moment beyond that."[13] Kelly directed and acted in it for two years, playing it in all the principal vaudeville houses throughout the country.[14] The play's moral apparently had immediate impact. When *Finders Keepers* played in Cincinnati, the theater management reported the return of an "unusual number" of lost articles.[15] Fifty years later, when Kelly was interviewed by *The New York Times* on the occasion of the revival of *The Show-Off*, he was especially proud of the fact that *"Finders Keepers* [was] still played a lot, mostly in schools as a good lesson for children."[16]

"A deadly serious playlet,"[17] *Finders Keepers* is the earliest example of the Kelly morality play; it is written to enforce the homely moral truth that "honesty is the best policy." Typically, Kelly creates for the dramatization of this truth an erring wife (Mrs. Aldrid), and a no-nonsense, moralizing husband (Mr. Aldrid). In the sketch, Mrs. Aldrid returns home from shopping with the announcement that she has found a purse with eight crisp new fifty-dollar bills in it. She feels she is entitled to the money, especially since the purse—"one of those little gold mesh purses"[18]—is entirely without identifying marks. There are a million purses just like it, she argues; and besides, she couldn't be certain she was returning the money to its proper owner: after all, who wouldn't be anxious to claim so much money?

Mrs. Aldrid's self-righteousness is undercut by the entrance of her neighbor, Mrs. Hampton, who agitatedly announces the loss of *her* purse which contained eight crisp new fifty-dollar bills. After she leaves, Mrs. Aldrid (evincing the stubbornness and meanness of several of Kelly's later matrons) suggests that Mrs. Hampton overheard her story and is only trying to get some easy money. Mrs. Aldrid's scheme is aborted, however, when she realizes that she doesn't have the purse; like Mrs. Hampton, she, too, lost her pocketbook. When Aldrid calls the department store, he is told that the person who found the pocketbook took all the money out of it before turning it in; and the unself-aware Mrs. Aldrid snaps, "Can you imagine anybody being that contemptible!" "I'm going to give you a lesson in honesty," Aldrid tells his wife, and he pays Mrs. Hampton with his own money which he gets from the top drawer of his bureau in which, conveniently, he has on hand eight crisp new fifty-dollar bills.

The play's machinery is clearly immature; for the dependence on coincidence, the convenient fact that the lost purse belongs to their neighbor, and the irony that the pocketbook-conscious Mrs. Aldrid should allow her pocketbook out of her sight for a second, are contrivances that bespeak the methods of a fledgling technician. But the moralizing tone, the character types, the inclusion of minute household details, the general fussiness of the characters and their surface politeness, and the continual questioning and cross-questioning, are all pure, if unpolished, Kelly.

Like several full-length Kelly plays, *Finders Keepers* is really about the education of a husband. Like Walter Craig after him, Eugene Aldrid lives in ignorance of the true nature of his wife; and the objective of the play is to enlighten him (and us). Aldrid, a part that Kelly wrote for himself, is an austere moralist. As *raisonneur*, Aldrid administers the play's lesson: "I'm going to give you a lesson in honesty," he says; and many of his male successors say the same thing in the later Kelly plays. "Your—attitude—in this affair to-night . . . has shown me that my wife is not *strictly* honest—for the sake of being so; and honesty is such a passion with me that, as far as you are concerned, life will never be the same again; because I could never absolutely *trust* you again. Never. I'm very sorry we found that out—I'm sorrier—than if I had lost a million dollars." This passion for honesty and moral integrity is the fundamental Kelly theme, and it is appropriate that the theme receives such central attention in this early play.

In addition to its instructive function, *Finders Keepers* is Kelly-like in its universalized character types; for Kelly emphasizes particularly the "averageness" of Mrs. Aldrid. "You're like a million other people in this world," Aldrid scolds her, "honest, as long as you don't *lose* anything by it; but as soon as you see where the principle of honesty is going to *cost* you a dollar, you begin to *hedge!*"

The play is also pure Kelly in structure as well as in theme and tone. It is appropriate that the first line in his first produced play is Mrs. Aldrid's "Heavens! five o'clock!", for Kelly's characters are invariably precise in such small matters as the correct time, train schedules, rudimentary household routine. (Mrs. Aldrid: "Did you come out on the four-fifty-three?") Like many later works (*Craig's Wife, The Deep Mrs. Sykes*, and *The Fatal Weakness* in particular), *Finders Keepers* is a play of questions: Where was the purse lost? At what time? What was in it? "Then you think it was somewhere between Blum's glove-counter and the bank steps that you lost it?"

There is also a curious prophetic appropriateness in that an

object—the purse—receives such prominent attention. As Mary
McCarthy has indicated, objects like pocketbooks and after-dinner
coffee cups are perennials in the Kelly canon, and they occupy a
position more exalted than that of mere theatrical machinery. When
Mrs. Aldrid is called upon to identify the contents of her pocketbook, she recites the list with reverence. True Kelly matron that she
is, she regards these minutiae as the ultimate reality of her life:
"Why, there's a silver vanity case—and a gold bracelet—with the
clasp broken—and a tax receipt, and a—sample of Georgette
Crepe, and a face veil, and a handkerchief, and two packages of
hairpins." In addition to the play's archetypal Kelly husband and
wife, the pocketbook and its contents also prefigure familiar "mem-
bers" of the playwright's dramatis personae.

IV   *The Flattering Word*

In his next sketch, *The Flattering Word*, Kelly again wrote for
himself a role as moral instructor. Eugene Tesh is an actor who plays
the part to the hilt—"You see I carry a cane now . . . Sign of an
actor"[19]; and, while he is playing Youngstown, he drops by to see an
old school friend. Like Aldrid, Tesh is the sententious sort whose
subject is the high purpose of the theater rather than honesty and
moral integrity. His friend Mary is married to Mr. Rigley, a minister who is "officially" opposed to the theater; but Tesh, wiser than
his adversary, changes the attitude of the unsuspecting minister
with "the flattering word": "Tell any man, woman or child that he
should be on the stage,—and you'll find him quite as susceptible as
a cat is to catnip." By telling Rigley about his physical resemblance
to Edwin Booth, Tesh catches him off guard; and the minister begins to overcome his disapproval of the theater.

The Flattering Word is Kelly's first play about the theater, and his
fondness and his respect for his profession are clearly indicated in it.
As Kelly's spokesman, Tesh tries to coax the minister away from his
bias by suggesting that the church and the theater are "simply
different branches of the same profession. Of course—I speak of the
institutions in their best sense." But, at the same time that the play
is Kelly's vindication of the theater, he attacks in it another of his
favorite subjects—provincial closed-mindedness:

Rigley: I'm afraid one doesn't see much of the best sense of the theater
nowadays, Mr. Tesh.
Tesh: One doesn't see anything at all, Mr. Rigley, if one doesn't look . . .

Conveniently, Tesh is performing in a play called *The Open Mind* which, as he informs his host, is about a spectator whose mind is opened by the theater:

Tesh: The theater gave him the only opportunity that one has—of seeing people in the dark.
Rigley: What did he *do* then—become an actor?
Tesh: No, no,—he became a minister.

Billed as a satire, *The Flattering Word* has provincial mentality as its target. Small-town people and vulgarians inevitably provoke the dramatist's displeasure, and his portraits in this play of poor Mrs. Zooker—who hasn't done much acting "these late years" and who wears "a get-up generally redolent of rummage sales and vanished vogues"—and of her daughter Lena, who is "one of those little fatties that doesn't care where she is or how she looks so long as there's refreshments," are quite harsh. Mrs. Zooker, a provincial stage mother, and Lena, who recites poetry, do not even reach the level of the rank amateur attained by the "company" in *The Torch-Bearers*. Kelly has no patience for the theatrical amateur, and he reveals his disdain through the condescending attitude of his professional actor Eugene Tesh. *The Flattering Word* is thus the true ancestor of *The Torch-Bearers*, Kelly's famous satire about those who are pathetically unequal to a career in the theater.

In the confrontation between big-city actor and small-town fools, *The Flattering Word* maintains a tone of superiority that some critics and audiences objected to in later Kelly work, particularly in *Philip Goes Forth*, a play about a would-be theater person who simply doesn't have "it." If the role of Tesh is not carefully played, it might easily seem officious and unlikable; but Kelly himself avoided the pitfall by wisely playing Tesh in a low key: "Mr. Kelly in the role of the star actor played with quiet distinction and good taste. A poseur with messages urging an open mind as regards the stage, he did not exaggerate or force his points which nevertheless went home and won converts through the flattering word."[20]

V *One of Those Things*

Finders Keepers and *The Flattering Word* enjoyed the longest runs of the one-acts. Kelly stayed with both sketches throughout their lengthy national tours, quietly relishing the roles of the superior message-bearers that he designed for himself. The other one-acts did not have such long lives, but all were at least moderately successful. There are "about ten others," according to Kelly, but he considered only "about half" worth publishing.[21]

One of Those Things, Smarty's Party, and *The Weak Spot* are even less conventional vaudeville fare than *Finders Keepers, The Flattering Word,* or *Poor Aubrey* (see p. 65). All three are written about standard subjects, but Kelly's conclusions frustrate popular expectation. *One of Those Things* offers a distinctly Kelly variation on *the* theatrical staple—the romantic triangle; but Kelly avoids the melodrama inherent in the situation—just as the cold-blooded heroine of his play avoids scenes. In this sketch, Dr. LeBold is having an affair with a patient, and Mrs. LeBold finds out about it. Because the LeBolds are characters in a Kelly play, they react to their dilemma in an individual way. Mrs. LeBold not only protects her rival, the adulterous Mrs. Scott, from a very suspicious Mr. Scott, but she also manages a reconciliation with her erring husband. Mrs. LeBold succeeds, that is, in avoiding social unpleasantness and in re-establishing the original status quo. (Forty years later, Mr. Sykes expresses the same conservative conviction—the advisability of maintaining a foundering marriage for the sake of appearance. Kelly does not always pursue such a conservative line, however: Mr. Craig breaks up house in *Craig's Wife,* and Mrs. Espenshade gives her husband his freedom in *The Fatal Weakness.*)

In her role as the Kelly *raisonneur,* Mrs. LeBold speaks for common sense when she tells her husband, "This is not a romantic age, Charles."[22] She is a cool, shrewd woman, and she will have no flare-ups: "I haven't come here to reproach you, or to plead for your return." Knowing her husband as she does, however, she feels that it would be unwise for him to take his freedom: " . . . you have a form of respectability that requires a certain anchorage in the conventions." She is a Kelly Puritan: "But unless you can reconcile yourself in the future to a more literal observance of those conventions, I shall be obliged to insist that you *take* your freedom . . . you haven't lost anything but a lot of time; and that's always lost when it's wasted on things that are insusceptible of conclusion. And this affinity business is one of those things." Marriages like theirs, she lectures, are "the portion of half the world . . . and I shall have the wisdom of disillusionment; as well as the consciousness of lots of company; for there are a million women exactly like me."

The ending is remarkable. After this cool discussion which touches the very center of their lives and after they have settled their future, the LeBolds lose themselves in Kelly small-talk:

Mrs. LeBold: You should have brought your overcoat today, Charles.
Dr. LeBold: It was warm when I left the house.
Mrs. LeBold: It's gotten very chilly.
Dr. LeBold: Yes, I know it has. I just came in a few moments ago. Have you all your things?
Mrs. LeBold: I think so. Have you the tickets? . . . By the way—there was a Mr. Strickland telephoned you here a few minutes ago—
Dr. LeBold: Yes, I know what that is.
Mrs. LeBold: He said he'd call you here Tuesday morning at ten o'clock.

And they go to the theater as if nothing very momentous has happened. Kelly does not suggest the peculiarity of this behavior—it is not as if his characters are consciously clinging to these small matters in order to avoid thinking about larger ones. The ending, in short, has more psychological reverberations than Kelly seems to be aware of; and this dead-pan absolutely straight-faced movement from discussion of the future of a marriage to fussy details about the weather, clothing, theater tickets, and phone messages is an archetypal moment in the Kelly Play.

VI Smarty's Party

Mrs. LeBold is a sensible woman, but she is hardly the type to warm an audience's heart. Mrs. Audenreid, in *Smarty's Party*, is even less of a crowd-pleaser; but clearly Kelly admires her and thinks she is morally correct. "Extremely aristocratic-looking," Mrs. Audenreid, like several Kelly matrons after her, returns from a trip to find that her house (a Park Avenue apartment, its drawing-room "done in shades of orchid") is *not* in order: her son Charles has taken advantage of her absence to marry Mildred, a girl not of his class. Incensed, Mrs. Audenreid, like any good Kelly character, is not one to turn the other cheek; she informs Charles that he is not in fact her son, but the son of one of her former servants, an irresponsible girl who had abandoned him on her employer's doorstep. Childless herself, Mrs. Audenreid decided to rear Charles but not to adopt him: "I was sentimental about you. And I rather *resented* the idea of any legalization of my relationship to you." Charles therefore finds himself disinherited, and he leaves his "mother's" house enraged—and penniless.

Smarty's Party follows the same unromantic course as *One of Those Things*. Kelly's heroine, a hard woman indeed, exhibits all the cold wrath of a woman scorned. But, since Kelly likes her, he provides a happy ending for her (she will marry a persistent suitor), and he tries to soften her character at the end by permitting her "a pang of bitter weeping"—a most uncharacteristic ending for a vaudeville sketch.

Kelly's sympathy for Mrs. Audenreid is also indicated by the way in which he characterizes her antagonist, Charles' new wife: "She's a perfect flapper, this one,—from the earrings to the slippers. . . . She's crafty, too, by the looks of her—in a thin-lipped way—and, somehow or another, rather common,—in the personal quality. . . . For, of course, her dress is entirely sleeveless, and much too short . . . a kind of all-night dancer type . . .her hair—so ruffed and burned that it's quite impossible to determine just which of its shades, if any, was the original one." Kelly's flavorful description scarcely conceals his moral disapproval of the flapper; moreover, Mildred is a fortune hunter who has pushed Charles into marriage.

Mildred, then, is guilty of two cardinal sins: she's one of those characters who doesn't make her own way and she is also, unforgivably, common. Kelly shares with Mrs. Audenreid an appreciation of the fact that society is divided into classes—and Mildred simply will not fit in her husband's class. As Joseph Wood Krutch has observed, "Mr. Kelly first delineates with cruel expertness the vulgarity of the adventuress and then, with a kind of savage delight, destroys her utterly."[23] Indeed, *Smarty's Party* is actually the earliest example of a Kelly trademark: the playwright's antipathy is centered on a female character. The most famous variation on the pattern is *Craig's Wife*, and like Mrs. Craig after her, Mildred's plans are frustrated, and the playwright superintends the downfall of both female characters with scarcely hidden glee.

Smarty's Party, then, is not a popularly conceived play. The fate of Mildred and Charles is harsher than most audiences would feel is necessary; and, with Mrs. Audenreid's acute consciousness of class, her prim morality, and her obsessive talk of mother love ("Simply a suggestion from a comparative stranger to you, and you were ready to exclude from consideration the woman who has been more to you than anybody else in the world"), she is hardly an endearing heroine. Kelly's tendency, evident here, to write in order to satisfy a highly personal and even rather ornery sense of moral justice excluded some of his later plays from popular and critical acceptance: writing as his own man, Kelly was not often on the same wavelength as his audience.

VII The Weak Spot

In 1945, Kelly wrote *The Deep Mrs. Sykes* which is about female intuition, but his first treatment of the subject occurs in his vaudeville sketch *The Weak Spot* in 1919. In the later play, Kelly regards intuition as a female foible, as something at which to scoff; in the vaudeville sketch, however, he allows for the possibility of intuition. In the sketch, Mrs. West is deeply, conventionally superstitious; Mr. West, the male Kelly scoffer, is skeptical. The events of the play, though, convince him of the possible foolhardiness of his opposition, and at the end of the play (unseen by his wife, of course) he throws salt over his shoulder after having accidentally spilled some. The change in his attitude has been brought about by Jenny, one of the most peculiar characters in the Kelly canon. Kelly's description of her suggests that, like all of his characters, she is "drawn from life": "a weird, poor creature, tall and spare . . . one of those almost mysterious figures that, on certain Saturdays, comes peddling notions to the women of the suburbs." But, if type she is, she is one that has passed out of American culture; and, as she appears in the sketch in her Salvation Army disarray, tells fortunes, bubbles biblical quotations, and spouts homely truths, she is like a ghost from a vanished rural Americana—at once the oddest, the least recognizable, and the best-spirited character in the Kelly pantheon.

Jenny reads Mrs. West's fortune: Mrs. West will hear of Mr. West's death—heart trouble—but there will be no grief. After Jenny leaves, the Wests in fact do receive word of Mr. West's "death." Mr. West, it turns out, had given his raincoat, with the usual personal effects in it, to a business associate, who half an hour later suffered a fatal heart attack. This coincidence unsettles West, and he is sufficiently convinced of Jenny's powers to consider at least the possibility that, after all, there may be something to superstition and "hunches."

Adhering to Kelly's notion of drama as moral instruction, *The Weak Spot* is written to impress the audience with the importance and the universality of superstition: "Everybody's superstitious— That's the weak spot in all of us." Jenny, who is entrusted with the

theme speech, elaborates: "Well, maybe you don't call it superstition; some people don't. Some people call it hunches and intuitions;
but it's all the same thing. It's the wisdom of the soul, that's what it
is. We all get flashes of it occasionally, but it's so hard to understand, that we say we don't believe it."

Jenny's speeches all have a religious fervor; her dialogue is, as we
have observed, flecked with biblical echoes: "You see, I took no
thought for my body, wherewith I should be clothed; and there, you
see, I am arrayed like a lily of the field." Though Kelly was religious,
religious questions do not appear directly in the plays. Of his work,
this curious one-act play about superstition is the most conspicuously spiritual.

The Weak Spot takes quite some time before it works itself
around to the fortune-telling passage and to the coincidental subsequent events. Casually structured, the play is really more interested in displaying the minutiae of its characters' lives than in its
overt subject of superstition. The first part of the sketch is a fine
example of the Kelly business in action: an abundance of inconse-
quential domestic conversation, generous doses of barbed Kelly
dialogue, and Mr. and Mrs. West showering each other with petty
gripes and dry sarcasm in a way that anticipates particularly the
squabbling Fisher household in *The Show-Off* and the wrangling
Mettingers in *Daisy Mayme*. This exchange of the Wests is an especially bright passage:

Mrs. West: You never heard of anybody throwing salt over their shoulder?
West: Nobody but you.
Mrs. West: Well, I wouldn't let anybody hear me say so if I were you;
they'll wonder where you were brought up.
West: I was brought up right here in this city, if anybody wants to know
where I was brought up. And in a much classier neighborhood than the one
you were brought up in.
Mrs. West: I've got a fine chance of having much chicken for dinner while
I'm married to you.
West: I guess I'd be all right if I could keep you running around from one
dog show to the other.
Mrs. West: You'll never be all right, kid, while your head's the shape it is.
West: You're only talking that way to discourage competitors.
Mrs. West: Ha!

When Jenny arrives, interrupting this connubial contentiousness,
the conversation becomes a veritable aria about things. Jenny sells

things, collects things, gives and receives things; and these things have personal histories: " . . . my hat. I only got it last week. A woman out on Wayne Avenue gave it to me. . . . She said her husband brought it to her from Dayton, Ohio, in 1912." Things define their owners: "Do you like this coat, Mrs. West? . . . A woman out in Tioga gave me this. She said it was her mother's . . . They're very rich people. She says her daughter has eleven pairs of shoes. . . But they're very nice people. It was through them that my husband got into Jefferson Hospital."

Though nominally a sketch about superstition, *The Weak Spot*, like all of Kelly's work, is about the American family preoccupied with, obsessed by, and subservient to possessions, objects, things: gloves, hats, scarves, pocketbooks, raincoats (and the contents of pocketbooks and raincoats), clasps (Mrs. West buys one from Jenny), shoes, forks and spoons, clocks, telephones. *The Weak Spot* is an inventory of the objects in the West household; and the Wests themselves, like all of Kelly's characters, are tied intimately to the material surfaces of their lives.

Considering the type of theater for which Kelly's one-acts were written, they are a unique achievement. Their special characteristics—the tart, dictaphonic yet slyly stylized dialogue; the domestic detail; the moralizing tendency; and the puritan zeal—are carried over into Kelly's ten full-length plays.

VIII   A La Carte

In 1927, Kelly interrupted his succession of increasingly stern full-length plays with his participation in a revue called *A La Carte*. Presented by Kelly's usual producer, Rosalie Stewart, *A La Carte* was intended as a *divertissement*—a light summer entertainment. It opened in July at a summer theater in Connecticut, and it was brought in to New York in late August. 1927 was late in the day for vaudeville (though the "official" end was the closing of the Palace as a two-a-day in 1932). Most of the critics felt *A La Carte* was too fragile to occupy a Broadway theater all by itself: it might have fared more profitably, they wrote, in its natural setting, one of the houses on the Keith-Orpheum circuit.

Kelly's contribution to the entertainment consisted of three sketches (which, unfortunately, he did not feel were worth publishing). Richard Watts' description makes the sketches sound like vintage Kelly: " . . . Mr. Kelly has provided lengthy cartoons of the middle classes at play that are not so far from the mood of his *Daisy Mayme*. . . . In none of them has Mr. Kelly attempted to build a punch line at the conclusion. He has sought his humor, instead, in characterization, in the satire of familiar types, in the general comedy of recognition. Though all of them seemed just a bit too long last night, the first two are filled with delightful and rather malicious observation."[24]

Kelly's sketches were, of course, the center of critical attention. Sandwiched among "discordant strutters, sentimentalities from the South, routine Spanish interludes, clog-dancers, jesting monologues and even a defiantly vivacious and humorless old-fashioned travesty,"[25] Kelly's sketches kept the revue from becoming the usual "musico-comico-girl-glorifying offering."[26] "While far too literary in flavor for the full appreciation of the average Broadway audience,"[27] the skits were commended for their "excellent taste" and for their scrupulous avoidance of the "standard smoking car jokes" of the blackout. Without "smut" and with "real wit and keen observation," Kelly provided "an eye and ear show" that filled "a long-felt want . . . a revue to which an entire family may go without disastrous consequences."[28]

With his customary side-stepping of the usual vaudeville fare, Kelly wrote three lampoons of the middle classes in which "nothing much happens" but which "cast the spell of actuality."[29] *The Hotel Porch* is a slice of "a gabby, fretful afternoon on a boarding-house verandah."[30] There are twelve characters on stage, and the management problems that this presents recalls Kelly's crowded stage in Acts I and II of *The Torch-Bearers*. "Deadly" in their humor, Kelly's group of average people "gabble and bluster banalities on the hotel porch."[31]

In *Between Numbers*, the second skit, Kelly returns to a theater milieu in a playlet that is a conversation, drenched in acid, between a prima donna, Miss Pine, and that Kelly perennial, the maid. Their exchange of scandal "on the circuit" sounds like a dry run for the barbed exchanges between Muriel Flood and her pert maid Hattie in *Reflected Glory*, Kelly's 1936 play of theatrical manners. Filled with theater jargon, *Between Numbers* was apparently too specialized for a general audience; "but when the dressing-room maid mixes her 'big time' jargon about minor tragedies on the road—about the player whose husband 'went out of his mind after a matinee in Duluth' and who 'took the body back to New York and opened cold at the Riverside'—even the uninitiated find themselves having a good time."[32] The third skit, *Daisies on the Green*, was a satire about the manners among lady golfers whose lack of expertise, apparently, is equivalent to that of the would-be actresses in *The Torch-Bearers*.

The skits in *A La Carte* were not without the Kelly sternness and the Kelly moral disapproval, but they did mark a departure from the increasingly unpopular direction of his writing. An interruption of his prestigious playwriting career, *A La Carte* represented Kelly's affectionate tribute to his training ground, the two-a-day.

CHAPTER 4

The Popular Plays

*T*HE *Torch-Bearers* (1922), *The Show-Off* (1924), and *Craig's
Wife* (1925) were all financial as well as artistic successes; and,
aside from his vaudeville sketches, these three plays were the only
hits Kelly ever had. Though the three plays are audience shows,
written in a popular range, they are at the same time personal plays
rather than mere box-office commodities. As is typical with Kelly,
the plays' subjects reflect the author's personal dislikes: in *The
Torch-Bearers*, Kelly satirizes provincial manners and amateur actors; *The Show-Off* more gently criticizes another Kelly *bête noir*,
the individual who does not make his own way in the world but
depends on others to carry his load for him; *Craig's Wife* flays a
recurrent Kelly type, the haughty, dominating, narrow suburban
matron. Silly women, freeloaders, frigid women—the plays offer a
sampling of Kelly's usual dramatis personae.

Even in these popular plays, Kelly writes with moral purpose;
and even in *The Show-Off*, his warmest play, he is not exactly
amiable; the play has much of the tart quality of the freeloader's
saucy mother-in-law. With an upper-middle-class setting and an icy
heroine, *Craig's Wife* is the most prominent of the three plays in
terms of Kelly's future development. Kelly never returned to the
slapstick humor of *The Torch-Bearers*—the comedy of his later plays
is not quite so broad—and, though he returned to the milieu of *The
Show-Off* in both *Daisy Mayme* and *Maggie the Magnificent*, his
thematic concerns are less in touch with the popular note and are
more conspicuously ornery and idiosyncratic. Kelly deliberately, it
seems, avoided using his gift for popular comedy; for his plays move
away from the broad humors of vaudevillian comedy to the more
refined sensibility of upper-class drawing rooms. Never writing
merely for fun, Kelly apparently wanted to be certain that his work
would never be labeled "common" or trifling—would never be
aimed simply for the "gigglers."

I   The Torch-Bearers

The Torch-Bearers, Kelly's first full-length play, sports ample evidence of the playwright's vaudeville experience;[1] and his later plays about theatrical types—*Philip Goes Forth* (1931) and *Reflected Glory* (1936)—are more sober variations on the theme and milieu of *The Torch-Bearers*. All three are plays about the theater by a playwright who respected the drama not only as a disciplined craft and as an art but also as something of a divine calling. Because the characters in *The Torch-Bearers* are amateurs who are attempting a task—the production of a play—for which they are conspicuously unsuited, they receive Kelly's stern reprimand. Fred Ritter, a man of impeccable common sense, speaks Kelly gospel when he lectures his errant wife and her friends: "I am . . . familiar . . . with a little remark Mr. Napoleon made on one occasion, a long time ago;—about the immorality of assuming a position for which one is unqualified."[2]

Kelly wrote the play, typically, not simply as disinterested entertainment—though it *is* great fun—but as *instructive* entertainment; and he laced his burlesque of little-theater amateurishness with the solemn treatise that if we are anything less than complete professionals, we should not participate in plays, for we will only make fools of ourselves and insult the art we are trying so helplessly to practice. Obeying the traditional function of its "satirical comedy" genre, then, *The Torch-Bearers* ridicules vanity and hypocrisy for purposes of moral correction.

Kelly establishes his moral norm by using many of the techniques of vaudeville farce and burlesque (the play is, in fact, more "vaudevillian" than any of his "real" vaudeville sketches); but he insists that *The Torch-Bearers* is "high comedy" and decidedly not farce. "I have no hand at farce. I'm not a farce director. I never could write a farce. I don't like farce, particularly its dependence on *double entendre*."[3] Kelly regarded the play as a *serious* comedy, and his closeness to his subject and his conviction of the high importance of his theme doubtless prompted both the harshness of his satire and his recourse in Act III to a clear underlining of his central idea.

In the action of the play, Mrs. J. Duro Pampinelli, the local self-styled *artiste* who takes it upon herself to direct a little theater production of *Dr. Arlington's Wife*, is a vain and silly woman; and Kelly satirizes her with little mercy. Kelly's full disapproval of Mrs. Pampinelli and her cohorts is unleashed in his sententious Act III.

After the impish fun of the disorganized rehearsal in Act I and the colossally abortive performance in Act II, the play settles down in Act III to a straightforward castigation of the ladies' follies. Heywood Broun complained: "The last act deals entirely with the rage of the husband against his wife because of her ineptness in the amateur entertainment. This is not the least amusing and it is hardly credible. In few States of the Union is bad acting listed as a crime."[4] Most of the critics, in fact, protested the darkening of the tone in the Act III confrontation between common sense and folly: "There is really no excuse for the vituperative remarks made by Fred Ritter . . . to her [Paula Ritter's] friends," scolded the anonymous reviewer for *The New York Evening Post*.[5] Newspaper reviewer Percy Hammond expressed a popular viewpoint when he wrote about Mrs. Pampinelli: "It is rather a cruel travesty of many a good and nervous lady, who though ill equipped for the function, volunteers to tend the flambeau of dramatic art."[6]

The "unpleasant" quality of Act III prefigures much of Kelly's later work. The audience-pleasing ambiance of Act I and II, in fact, becomes less and less Kelly's mode, and it is the sardonic atmosphere of Act III that comes to dominate his later work.

But Kelly's missionary zeal and his evident dislike of the type which Mrs. Pampinelli represents do not diminish the high-spiritedness, the sly, wicked fun, of the first two acts. The Act I rehearsal scene and the Act II performance amply demonstrate Kelly's reliance on theater business and on making "points." Both acts, in effect, are comprised of a series of vaudeville turns. "The day after . . . *The Torch-Bearers* [opened], the late David Belasco . . . came to Kelly . . . 'You gave me a pretty bad turn at the opening last night . . . Do you know you had about twelve people, moving and landing points at the same time? Where did you learn to do that?' 'Vaudeville,' said Kelly, giving credit to a fine school."[7]

Act I, a beautifully orchestrated compendium of traditional theater business, opens with the indispensable maid whose expository chatter sets the play in motion. By telling Fred Ritter, who has just returned from a business trip, about the rehearsal to be held in his living room that night, Jenny alerts the audience to the play's situation. From this quintessentially *theatrical* opening, the act advances with an unending series of bits and pieces of business. Paula Ritter asks Jenny for a glass of water, which Jenny dutifully brings in on a silver tray. For no reason, except to provide a kind of grace note,

Paula asks Jenny to go to the top of the stairs "and see if I left the lights burning in my room?" This type of incidental, mundane detail is a typical Kelly ploy; and, while such respect for detail may seem to give the plays realistic texture, it in fact is the basis for the plays' special, peculiar stylization.

One by one, the participants in the amateur theatrical enter; engage in bantering small talk; and move in complicated, interlocking patterns about Paula's handsomely appointed living room. The sole concession to plot is the recurrent reference to the death of Clara Sheppard's husband and Paula's eleventh-hour replacement of the widow who was to have been their star. Kelly's interest, here as elsewhere, is in revealing his characters' foolishness rather than in advancing his story line; for he gives each of his characters particular activities suggestive of the type they represent. Mrs. Pampinelli intones, expostulates, frets, and orders. She is accompanied by Mr. Spindler, her "lead-pencil-bearer extraordinary," who toadies unceasingly to her ladyship's opinions and whims. Mrs. Nelly Fell, the promptress, is the eternal clubwoman, beminked, bouffanted, chauffeur-driven. Her coy flirtations with Fred Ritter ("You bold thing!"), which prevent her from attending to her official duties, provide a droll counterpoint to the center-stage rehearsal. The delightfully named Mr. Huxley Hossefrosse, the leading man, is vain about his deep-barreled voice, but he is forever "up"in his lines. The company, such as it is, is completed by Teddy ("his type is always to be found draped upon the banisters or across the pianos in the houses of the rich"); Florence McCrickett, the earnest, flat-voiced second woman; and Mr. Twiller, the second man, who is plagued by a recalcitrant false moustache. Such a crowded stage and such simultaneous business require the most exact timing; and Kelly is certainly correct in maintaining that *The Torch-Bearers* can only be played by "an absolutely professional cast, which must be entirely subject to the director."[8]

Act II is even more intricate, for two activities occur simultaneously: the performance of *Dr. Arlington's Wife*, of which the audience hears pertinent snatches at perfectly timed intervals; and the backstage preparations, altercations, and upheavals. The "on-stage" performance is a series of calamities: everyone manages to trip on his entrance (Mrs. Pampinelli: "You can trip on exits, that's not so bad, but not on entrances"); poor Mr. Twiller's moustache falls off, piecemeal; neither pen nor ink is on the doctor's desk, and both are urgently needed for purposes of plot advancement. The telephone buzzer has periodic attacks of temperament, not working when needed, and buzzing incessantly at unwelcome moments. The stage door gets stuck; Hossefrosse is "up" in his lines; and, when Nelly gives him the wrong cue, she and Mrs. Pampinelli yell at him through the shaky partition; Paula doesn't talk loudly enough; Teddy, dazed by the absent pen and ink, faints when he leaves the stage; and Spindler, who manages with sublime completeness to miss every one of his cues, rushes him to the drug store. As a final blow, the curtain gets stuck at the end of the curtain calls, just as Mrs. Pampinelli is about to make her sweeping entrance in response to the tumultuous pleas for "Director! director!"[9]

The mayhem, the burlesque, the physicalized, visual humor are all vestiges of Kelly's vaudeville days:

Of vaudevillian habit are one or another of his comic tumults—din, helter-skelter, the rattle of loud and inchoate confusion, the fun-making of the indispensable fall. Vaudevillian again is not a little of the characters' chatter. Time and again they merely answer back—obviously; while the scorer in the stall marks up one more "repartee."[10]

The play is full of points, and in each of the three acts the players make their points with the accuracy of sharpshooters. No play of the year is so well punctuated with laughter. . . . [11]

The play's first two acts—the rehearsal and the performance—are theatrical showpieces, and they could well stand on their own. In fact, the ill-fated performance in Act II had been the basis of a Kelly one-act, *Mrs. Ritter Appears*, a twenty-minute skit that Kelly did not feel was worth publishing. Both acts have the quick impact of vaudeville sketches—in fact, they conform to the conventions of vaudeville comedy in a way that Kelly's one-acts do not. "[Kelly] writes his play in three installments. . . . He sets them in sequence, like the items in an exhibition; but little or nothing else binds them together. . . . they [the characters] are merely on view in variously amusing circumstances, like a 'strip' drawn across the stage rather than set in a comic supplement."[12] But, even if Acts I and II seem like revue skits, Act III clearly depends on what precedes it; without exposure to the ladies' foolishness, Fred Ritter's displeasure in Act III would be altogether arbitrary.

What some of the critics found especially objectionable was Kelly's blithe circumvention of the rules. *The Torch-Bearers* violates conventional three-act structure; it is decidedly not a well-made play. As Kenneth Macgowan observed: "Brander Matthews and Aristotle would scoff at *The Torch-Bearers*. George M. Cohan and Professor Baker would scowl at George Kelly. The odd little thing that crept into the 48th Street Theater last night smashes most of the rules for works of dramatic art and all of the canons of Broadway success."[13]

Establishing its own rules, *The Torch-Bearers* is an altogether personal play despite its seemingly conventional reliance on the paraphernalia of slapstick, burlesque, and type characters. As always, Kelly writes about types; his characters are intended to be immediately recognizable. But Kelly's treatment of types, like his dramatic structure and his moralizing tone, is decidedly original.[14]

As Alexander Woollcott noted, Kelly depends on "the shock of recognition" both for the play's situation and for its characterizations: "There is said to be a morbid, sardonic old man living in Unadilla Forks, New York, who never appeared in amateur dramatics. But with that single possible exception all adults in this State will find something in their own past to make them both squirm and roar with laughter."[15] The special characteristic of Kelly's achievement is that "he has succeeded in some mysterious fashion in transmuting his material . . . 'base' enough, obvious enough, if the truth must be told—into a sort of universality."[16]

It is certainly true that the material lacks elevation, and yet Kelly's treatment of it has such style that critics sought for parallels in classic comedy. For example, Carl Carmer asserted that "Mrs. Pampinelli bids fair to be as immortal as Mrs. Malaprop and for much the same reasons. She is a summation of a type."[17] And to Robert Allerton Parker, "There is certainly an engaging likeness to Moliere's comedy of the learned ladies in *The Torch-Bearers*. Paula Ritter, Nelly Fell, and Mrs. J. Duro Pampinelli are contemporary incarnations of Armande, Belise, and Philaminte. . . . Kelly's play awakens an appetite for productions of Congreve and Moliere."[18]

The Torch-Bearers is typical of Kelly in its precarious straddling of the popular and the high-brow; for, if the play has echoes of classic comedy, it also has much humbler antecedents, as one writer has indicated: "Years ago in Daly's Theater, the volatile Rosina Vokes and her excellent company were wont to convulse their audiences in a screamingly funny farce called *A Pantomime Rehearsal*, in which a group of unskilled amateurs went through a rehearsal of a charity performance. That same idea, in a newer, fresher guise, is capitally developed in George Kelly's little comedy."[19] Kelly was familiar with Miss Vokes' company from his vaudeville days—indeed, he was better acquainted with her work than with that of Moliere, Congreve, or Sheridan.

Kelly also knew another "low-brow" predecessor to *The Torch-Bearers*, Clare Kummer's 1920 farce, *Rollo's Wild Oat*. Mrs. Kummer's entertainment has very much the same structure as Kelly's play: the befuddled rehearsal and agitated preliminaries of Act I, the catastrophic Act II performance, the more sober Act III resolution. In the last act, Rollo turns his back on amateur theater and accepts the practical life—marriage and partnership in his reactionary grandfather's solid steam-pump business. Mrs. Kummer's play is charming, but it lacks the rhythm and the splendid command of detail of Kelly's play, as well as its moral fervor. The characters' defection from the theater in *Rollo's Wild Oat* seems merely a nod to convention; Mrs. Kummer, that is, ends her play merely to end it. Unlike Kelly, she is not writing from a deep conviction that engaging in work for which we are unsuited is a moral offense. Kelly's conviction makes his play far more idiosyncratic and crotchety than Mrs. Kummer's pleasing, but essentially disinterested, comedy.

What also personalizes *The Torch-Bearers* is Kelly's working out of a miniature *Poetics*, particularly through the sublimely misinformed statements of Mrs. Pampinelli. Mrs. Pampinelli and her disciple, Paula Ritter, speak Kelly gospel—in reverse. When Paula tells Fred that Mrs. Pampinelli "tells us where to go, you know, on the stage,—so we won't be running into each other," she is revealing Kelly's disapproval of the director as traffic cop. Poor misguided Mrs. Pampinelli also wants broad, pictorial gestures from her actors; she wants sweeping entrances, studied poses, and a few tears ("within the limits of the characterization, of course"). In fact, she sponsors all the tricks of the trade that Kelly's own muted, detailed, naturalistic direction tried to circumvent.

Kelly adds emphasis to his attack by having Mrs. Pampinelli misdirect his own dry, understated one-act *One of Those Things* (here entitled, more melodramatically, *Dr. Arlington's Wife*). Kelly's play adroitly sidesteps the conventional consequences of its romantic triangle, but Mrs. Pampinelli altogether mistakes the play's tone. She tries for a fevered pitch: "It seems to me—that it is there—that she makes her big plea, for her boys, for her home,—for every woman's home. And even though that plea *is* made in the form of a threat,—somehow or other—I seem to hear her saying, sub-vocally, of course, 'In God's *name, don't* make it necessary for me to do this thing!' " And Mrs. Pampinelli concludes this speech, Kelly notes, "rather dramatically, her arms outstretched."

Kelly's thematic emphasis also gives the material a personal touch. He clearly intends to satirize the little-theater movement: "There was a great flowering of little theater groups at the time. Everyone who had a chicken coop had a little theater," Kelly said.[20] But he deliberately avoids the suggestion that the movement "was owing to any coalition of social forces as Kenneth Macgowan did when he wrote the history of the movement";[21] he's interested in lambasting amateur actors. In summary, Kelly is simply not interested in social implications or in large socio-cultural generalizations.

Kelly is not interested in the problem of women's rights either. Clearly, he feels these women belong in the home, performing their traditional roles and providing comfort for their businessmen-husbands. Kelly does not entertain for a moment the possible seriousness of Mrs. Fell's "Oh, I suppose it must be *very* difficult for the marvelous male, to suddenly find himself obliged to bask in the reflected glory of a mere wife," or of Mrs. Pampinelli's even more obviously satirized pronouncements:

Husbands are not always particular about telling the truth—where the abilities of their wives are concerned. If *I* had listened to the promptings of my own soul, instead of to my husband . . . I should in all probability be one of the leading figures in the American Theater today; . . .

Only remember this, Paula,—there will be actresses when husbands are a thing of the past; . . .

I think that the question of whether to be or not to be an actress is one that every woman must, at some time or other in her life, decide for herself.

The battle of the sexes is a basic impetus for most of Kelly's work; and though the subject is treated lightly in this play, there are nonetheless indications of elemental male-female antagonism. Under *The Torch-Bearer's* popular comic surface, a not so amiable satire of female follies exists.

In 1935, the play was made into a film, *Doubting Thomas*, which served as a vehicle for Will Rogers; but placing the character of the husband center stage wrenched the play out of its initial shape. The husband's role is intrusive in the first place, and giving him the star role saps much of the comic energy. In addition, Rogers' "homely wit and genial philosophizing," his "good old American family sentiment," and his incarnation of "the very spirit of middle-class wisdom" are foreign to the spirit of Kelly's acerbic, not-altogether-congenial, wise-cracking *raisonneur*.[22] But the film was graced by Alison Skipworth, who repeated her triumphant impersonation of Mrs. Pampinelli, and by Billie Burke, who was fittingly type-cast as the wife turned fledgling actress. "As the screen's champ fluttery comedienne," reported *Variety*, "Miss Burke's a natural for a part calling for more fluttering than is found in a flock of pigeons."[23]

II   The Show-Off

The Show-Off, Kelly's greatest popular and critical success, received universal praise and has had more productions than any of his other plays. If Kelly is known at all today, it is as the author of this play; if his work is included in survey courses on American drama, it is inevitably *The Show-Off* that is read. And *The Show-Off* earned Kelly the mistaken reputation of being a Realistic playwright. This particular play of the domestic upsets of a very average family of a very average Philadelphia suburb *is* a splendid example of American Realism, but no other Kelly play is written in quite the same key. The Kelly business is present, along with the recurrent themes and the underlying Puritanism; but the materials are all subtly transmuted into giving the appearance of a Realistic "audience show." With the arguable exception of *Craig's Wife*, Kelly was never again to deal with such popular material in such a seemingly popular, non-idiosyncratic manner.

In *The Show-Off*, Kelly, as usual, is concerned more with his characters than with his thin plot. The show-off bursts into the sober Fisher household, first as Amy's suitor, then as visiting son-in-law, and finally (after Pa Fisher's death) as a permanent guest. His horse laugh, his quips, and his colloquial endearments nearly drive Mrs. Fisher to distraction. A perennial bungler, Aubrey manages to have a car accident on the day Pa Fisher suffers a fatal stroke. Aubrey is self-deluding, and he has convinced himself that he's a "man on the way up," even though he's only a thirty-two-dollar-a-week clerk at the Pennsylvania Railway. But his bravado *does* work at the end when he manages to talk his brother-in-law Joe's invention—a solution for the prevention of rust in iron and steel—into a one-hundred-thousand-dollar contract.

The bickering between the show-off and his mother-in-law is the play's main concern, and their contrasting personalities, rather than the attenuated plot, provide the play's charm and its principal interest. Though Kelly relegates his plot to the sidelines, *The Show-Off* is nonetheless a well-made play that obeys the conventional pattern of exposition, climax, and resolution. Reviewing the 1967 revival, Clive Barnes noted that, "unlike so many lesser well-made plays earlier in this century that glorified in their technical devices, Mr. Kelly's art is largely to conceal art."[24] That *The Show-Off* seems like a Realistic play is in fact no small accomplishment, considering Kelly's reliance on a number of altogether stock theatrical effects; indeed, "the events have considerable antique value, including a father carried off by a stroke, a will, an invention that brings riches, a surprise pregnancy and the turning of a worm, so to speak, at the very end."[25]

Like *The Torch-Bearers*, *The Show-Off* ridicules its characters; and, in the same way as in the former play, Kelly's success depends on "the shock of recognition." Everyone knows an Aubrey Piper, the perennial boaster, braggart, blowhard, and buffoon; the would-be con artist driven by get-rich-quick schemes; the guy who believes in the cult of personality. "Make 'em laugh and you'll get everyone on your side" is his motto. Kelly's treatment of the show-off is his most conspicuous success in bringing a flat character to life. Kelly himself attributed the play's long-lived impact to the fact that his Aubrey Piper is "a universal type; every office has one. I knew one in Philadelphia worse than Aubrey,—a good steady man but a complete fool."[26] At the time of the play's opening in 1924, Kelly had said, "Anyone that has an eye for the social scene must have encountered in his experience any number of Aubrey Pipers. . . . Something of a subconscious observation of a type very prevalent in the life of our day . . . found expression in dramatic form."[27] Aubrey was so exact an incarnation of an American character that he "became part of the language, a synonym for a self-delusive braggart." (Kelly's other type character who similarly rose to classic stature was, of course, Harriet Craig, "a synonym . . . for a destructive, materialistic wife.")[28]

On a less spectacular, but no less accurate scale, the characterization of Aubrey's chief antagonist, his mother-in-law Mrs. Fisher, is also a shrewd portrait "taken from life." Mrs. Fisher is the embodiment of the long-suffering wife and mother who must balance her books carefully in order to stretch her workingman husband's modest salary as far as possible. Like Fred Ritter in *The Torch-Bearers*, Mrs. Fisher is another of Kelly's common-sensical scoffers; and Mrs. Fisher is no more patient with Aubrey's shenanigans than Ritter is with his wife's misdirected thespianism.

Kelly's own ambivalent reaction to his two characters gives them dimension. Our responses to Aubrey and Mrs. Fisher are also complex and shifting; and, because we like them at times and dislike them at other times, the characters seem life-like, deep. We respond to Aubrey as being boisterous and parasitical, but kind-hearted, and to Mrs. Fisher as being stern and narrow-minded, but also practical and wise. Mrs. Fisher's daughter Clara is right when she says about Aubrey: "She [Amy] might have taken worse, Mom. He works every day, and he gives her his money; and nobody ever heard of him looking at another woman." And Aubrey is right about himself when he tells Amy, immediately after she has received news of her father's death: "Don't let it get you, Honey—you have nothing to regret; and nothing to fear. The Kid from West Philly'll never go back on you,—you know that, don't you, Baby?" And Mrs. Fisher is right when she complains that Aubrey is silly; he talks too much; he makes up tall stories; and he doesn't know half the time what he is saying.

Is Aubrey, then, "preposterous?"[29] Is he "so boorishly offensive that he is positively fascinating . . . offensively attractive, obnoxiously fascinating?"[30] Is he "an empty exhibitionist, an adenoidal, gaping moron?"[31] Or is he "a lovable creature despite his obnoxious traits?" Underneath the braggadocio, is there "warmth" and "a quality of fineness?"[32] The answer is that Aubrey is both lovable and a nuisance. He is both endearing and alienating, and his creator both likes him for his good qualities and dislikes him for his foolishness.

Kelly's own attitude to Aubrey is clouded by the surprise ending in which he allows the character to succeed in a shrewd business deal in which he doubles his brother-in-law's earnings from his invention. In response to this twist, are we supposed "to chuckle, thinking there may be something to Aubrey after all?"[33] Or is the triumph of Aubrey Piper designed to suggest that "big business is compounded of bluff, and theatricality, and bragging, and the mouthing of sententious proverbs?"[34] Most likely, the end of *The Show-Off* represents an uncharacteristic relaxation of Kelly's moral vigilance; for Aubrey's success is a clear-cut, audience-pleasing gesture.

Heywood Broun expresses exactly the sort of audience response Kelly reconciled himself to appeasing: "We didn't actually want to see the braggart here get his just deserts. In fact along about the middle of the play we grew a little uneasy and felt that the playwright was pursuing the young man with too much venom. . . . We found that we didn't want unswerving truth. We wanted the theater to take hold of life and twist it just a little nearer to heart's desire."[35] At the expense of "a really logical development of the theme," then, Kelly has allowed Aubrey an implausible coup; and Joseph Wood Krutch felt that Kelly's "sentimental blurring of the conclusion . . . renders the play as a whole so ambiguous that it might almost be taken as a 'success story' after the manner of Winchell Smith."[36] Kelly was never again to be liable to the charge of sentimentality; nor was he to go "soft" on one of his characters. In the rest of his work, an erring character is pursued with relentless fervor.

Though Mrs. Fisher may not be the audience favorite, she doubtless had Kelly's approval. Resourcefully economical, both preaching and living the sober, responsible life, Mrs. Fisher is a self-aware character; she sees life "hard" if she does not exactly see it "deep." Like the husband in *The Torch-Bearers*, she often speaks good common sense: "It's silly to try to make an impression of any kind," she counsels Aubrey, "for the only one that'll be made'll be the right one,—and that'll make itself." But she has an awfully narrow view of the world, and her aims are safe and life-denying. For example, she makes this sour speech:

Mrs. Fisher: There's nothing can be done by *anything*, Clara,—when once the *main* thing is done. And that's the marriage. That's where all the trouble starts—gettin' married.
Clara: If there were no marriages, there'd be no world.
Mrs. Fisher: Well, what if there wouldn't? Do you think it'd be any worse than it is now? I think there'll be no world pretty soon, anyway, the way things are goin'. A lot of whiffets gettin' married, and not two cents to their names. . . . You're about the only one I've heard talkin' about love *after* they were married. It's a wonder to me you have a roof over you; for they never have, with that kind of talk.

Clara's prophecy—"it isn't always the person that makes the bed that lies in it.—Very often somebody else has to be in it"—hangs like a shroud over the play. According to the Kelly code, Mrs. Fisher earns top honors because she assumes responsibility for Amy's and Aubrey's mistakes, because she owns the house that shelters them, and because she understands the value of a dollar. She does not escape Kelly's satiric thrusts, however; he is aware of her narrowness and her prejudices (she doesn't like Italians and Jews) just as he is aware of Aubrey's *joie de vivre*. Mrs. Fisher is occasionally likable, but she has the underlying rigidity that marks many of Kelly's later characters and that emanates also from the playwright.

Aubrey, Mrs. Fisher, the ambiance of the Fisher household—all charm the audience by their verisimilitude. Yet another of the play's reflections of contemporary life is its comic situation of the struggling and mismanaging young couple (Aubrey and Amy) who must move in with Amy's mother in order to avoid total catastrophe. "The problem of marriage among the young and poor interested me," Kelly said;

I knew that there were many young couples living around in attics whose marriages were doomed to destruction. I heard about some of them by talking to my mother's housekeeper and to maids in the homes of relatives and friends of mine. I was constantly hearing about a young girl in the same social set as *The Show-Off*, who was planning to return to the parental roof because she was tired of trying to make twenty-five dollars a week do the work of one hundred dollars. When the first glamor of love and marriage vanished, those poor innocents had nothing to sustain them. Devoid of intellectuality, wisdom, humor, struggling to keep their attic homes going, the mediocrity of their existence seemed appalling to me. That's what prompted me to write a play about them.[37]

As his statement of purpose suggests, Kelly's own observation about his work hardly coincides with popular opinion; no one thought *The Show-Off* was primarily (or even secondarily) an object lesson to young marrieds, and yet Kelly clearly regarded the situation of Aubrey and Amy, who are too poor to make their own way, as a word of warning: they should not get married until they could afford it. Ever the moral instructor, observing his characters from a distance, Kelly created Aubrey and the Fishers in the same ironic spirit that he presented *les femmes savantes* in *The Torch-Bearers*.

The Show-Off, then, is essentially a satire, which means that all the claims for the play's photographic Realism are wide of the mark. As social satirist, Kelly *heightened* his characters' follies in order to stress his paternalistic disapproval; and, though *The Show-Off* may look like life itself, it is composed of materials emphasized for satiric intent. Like virtually all of Kelly's work, *The Show-Off* represents a precarious mixture of genres and viewpoints: "It is satire of the most savage and penetrating sort even though the playwright smiles as he slashes."[38] And yet "you are less than discerning if you fail to feel the pathos and pity of the play."[39] It is perhaps "more a comedy of farce than legitimate comedy, for all it holds closely to its author's classification as a transcript of life."[40] And yet "the Russians of Moscow have been scarcely more successful in creating the illusion of reality in the theater."[41] The play provides "a curious sensation of being an invisible visitor in the Fishers' cozy home."[42] "A shrewd lampoon,"[43] it contains "the subconscious tragedy of the ever reaching for the unattainable."[44]

Kelly doesn't give his play tragic emphasis, but Aubrey's belief in salesmanship and his reliance on a "marketable" personality is an early anticipation of Arthur Miller's Willy Loman in *Death of a Salesman*. Kelly was certainly aware of the tragic possibilities of his material: "The opportunities for young men suggest to the unqualified achievements beyond the reaches of their souls, and herein is the tragedy."[45] *The Show-Off* manages "to talk about a death in the family and daughter Clara's loveless marriage between comic developments";[46] more—its comic texture remains intact despite the introduction of such elements as Mr. Fisher's death and Clara's unresponsive husband. Act II contains an especially daring juxtaposition. The two events of the act are Pa Fisher's death and Aubrey's foolish car accident; but tragedy and farce commingle beautifully, and the play's light texture remains unblemished.

The hesitations and backtrackings, the overlappings and repetitions, of Kelly's dialogue give the play its vitality. Alexander Woollcott astutely commented that Kelly's language is "humdrum patois reproduced slyly and with theatrical cunning."[47] Robert Benchley, another alert Kelly critic, was also accurate when he wrote that "The way in which every-day small talk and idioms are strung together, with scarcely a wisecrack or a gag-line to lend artificial brilliance, is just about as smooth a piece of work as we ever remember seeing."[48] And the anonymous review in *The World* which suggested that Kelly's dialogue surpasses O'Neill's was certainly well-founded:

> When O'Neill first came before the theatrical public . . . it was said again and again that here was a dramatist who had caught the flavor of the American language and brought it to the stage. The characters in O'Neill's plays were not burdened by the false and artificial tradition of speeches . . . By now . . . a number of playwrights have quite excelled O'Neill in the faithful reproduction of American speech. . . . Indeed, we rather think that Mr. Kelly shows a deeper comprehension of American life than O'Neill has yet achieved.[49]

For example, homely, yet quietly stylized rhythms characterize the quintessentially Kelly-like exchange that opens *The Show-Off*:

Clara: There's some of that candy you like.
Mrs. Fisher: Oh, did you bring me some more of that nice candy? I never got a taste of that last you brought.
Clara: Why not?
Mrs. Fisher: Why,—Lady Jane took it away with her down to the office, and never brought it back. She sez the girls down there et it. I sez, "I guess you're the girl that et it." She sez she didn't, but I know she did.
Clara: Well, I hope you'll keep that out of sight, and don't let her take that too.
Mrs. Fisher: Oh, she won't get her hands on this, I can promise you that. Let her buy her own candy if she's so fond of it.
Clara: She won't *buy* much of anything, if she can get hold of it any *other* way.
Mrs. Fisher: Oh, isn't that lovely! Look Clara—Don't that look nice?
Clara: Yes, they do their candy up nice.
Mrs. Fisher: That looks just like Irish point lace, don't it? I think I'll put that away somewhere,—in a book or something. My, look at all the colors—look Clara—did you ever see so many colors?
Clara: It's pretty, isn't it?
Mrs. Fisher: It's beautiful—seems a pity to spoil it. Do you want a bit of it, Clara?
Clara: Not now, Mom.
Mrs. Fisher: I think I'll take this pink one here. I *like* the pink ones. Mind how they all have this little fancy paper around them. You'd wonder they'd bother, wouldn't you?—just for a bit of candy. That's nice candy, isn't it?
Clara: Yes, *I* like bonbons.
Mrs. Fisher: I do too—I think I like them better than most anything. I'm sorry these are not all bonbons.
Clara: They *are* all bonbons. There's nothing else in there.

Mrs. Fisher: Oh, are they!—I thought only the pink ones were the bonbons.
Clara: No, they're all bonbons.
Mrs. Fisher: Well, that's lovely. I can eat any one of them I like, then, can't I?

This passage is delightfully "scored." The repetitions, the alternations between question and statement, and the exclamations have rhythm and balance; everything is carefully pointed and yet everything seems quite lifelike. This opening, with its clearly marked beginning, middle, and end, is a miniature aria; and yet it is linked to character (Clara's wistfulness; Mrs. Fisher's perkiness) and milieu. The entire play is built of just such precise verbal turns. Like the characters and like the structure of the play itself, the Kelly dialogue is familiar but distinctive; seemingly natural, it is actually delicately stylized. As Mary McCarthy has so accurately observed, a Kelly play "is not like anything else while on the surface it resembles every play one has ever been to."[50]

Like *The Torch-Bearers*, *The Show-Off* was expanded from a vaudeville sketch, *Poor Aubrey*. Critics were quick to detect the play's vaudeville origins and characteristics:

The influence of the writer's past experience was more marked than ever. . . . Aubrey Piper, like many a "single turn" actor in vaudeville, begins to talk before he enters and his preliminary off-stage noises are calculated to put his readers into a hilariously receptive mood. . . . Though a little less subtle the method of this is much the same as that of Ruth Draper in her beautifully observed impersonations. Kelly's Piper would be as alive and as utterly convincing . . . were he alone on a monologist's platform.[51]

[The play is] full of vaudeville "gags" if you please. . . . The principal character is a low comedian, a "type" . . . probably the most pronounced all-around damn fool since "Clarence" . . . Kelly knows, just as his brother, the Virginia Judge knows, when he so cunningly mingles hokum with sympathy in his negro and Tad characters of monolog.[52]

Aubrey's opening speech certainly has the flourish and the showmanship of a vaudeville turn. Richly colloquial, lively and sassy, it is an actor's dream:

Stay right where you are, folks, right where you are. Just a little social attention,—going right out again on the next train. There you are, Mother.

(Aubrey turns from the mirror and indicates his reflection with a wide gesture.) Any woman's fancy, what do you say? Even to the little old carnation. Come on, Amy, step on the United Gas out there; customer in here waiting for the old aqua pura. Man's got to have something to drink—how about it, Pop? You'll stay with me on that, won't you? Yes, sir. I want to tell those of you who have ventured out this evening, that this is a very pretty little picture of domestic felicity. Father reading,—Mother knitting; but then, Mama is always knitting. And little old Tommy Edison over here, working eighteen hours a day to make the rich man richer and the poor man poorer. What about it, Popcorn? (Slaps him on the back) Shake it up! Right or raving?

Like the other Kelly one-acts, *Poor Aubrey* is more genteel than the usual vaudeville routine *despite* Aubrey's brash vigor. A visit from an old friend of Amy's provides the sole dramatic action in the skit. When Marion's visit offers Aubrey the chance to reveal himself, he gives her the same "line of gab" about his work, his prospects, and his possessions that he delivers in a more elaborated version in the full-length play. He proudly says that he's a bigwig at the Pennsylvania Railroad, that he owns this fine house (and he had trouble getting it since competition was keen), that his car is "laid up" for a little "fixin'." A real peacock, he wears a carnation, and he is self-conscious about his toupee. The fuss about the wig, the fact that Marion Brill's husband is a wig maker, the tendency for Aubrey's wig to fall off at inopportune moments—these details are pitched on the rather obvious level of farce incongenial to the rest of the skit.

Poor Aubrey is sparked by the antagonism between Aubrey and Mrs. Fisher, who is an even meaner-spirited woman in her first presentation than her more famous play version; her conversation is a blend of petty gossip and self-pitying laments about illness and family misfortunes. *Poor Aubrey* is really one long ingenious conversational exchange—polite chit-chat about Marion's husband's flu, about Marion's muff, about the death of Amy's father three years ago at Christmas, about the neighborhood (different views on this subject from the show-off and his mother-in-law), and about the virtues of Atlantic City as a bathing resort. When Mrs. Fisher enters about mid-way through Marion's visit, the whole repertoire of small talk is politely repeated: the social niceties called into play by Marion's visit are observed with solemn, ritualized decorum.

The Show-Off enjoyed the full success that *The Torch-Bearers* never quite achieved. It ran for 571 performances, was revived for 119 performances in 1932, was produced in 1937 by the Federal Theater with an all-black cast, and was one of the Phoenix Theater's most solid achievements when it was mounted in 1967. The New York run was followed by a national tour; Helen Hayes played Mrs. Fisher; and those critics who had been around long enough to remember agreed that this role was her most rewarding one since *Victoria Regina* thirty years before. The Phoenix Theater had enjoyed one of its major successes in its 1966 staging of *You Can't Take It With You;* and some of the warmth, coziness, and general goodwill of the Kaufman and Hart comedy were mistakenly introduced into Kelly's decidedly less amiable domestic scene.[53] Sugar-coated or not, however, the Kelly dialogue sounded marvelously fresh. Like *The Torch-Bearers*, *The Show-Off* has been a staple in summer-stock theaters; and the Broadway revival spurred country-wide stock and repertory productions. The play's reputation as a minor American classic seems assured, but its reputation as an affectionate portrait of family life in that mythic period of the 1920's is a misrepresentation of the satiric spirit in which the play was written.

The Show-Off has been made into a film three times; and, like all the film versions of Kelly's plays, the original Kelly tone was coarsened by Hollywood. The first version, in 1926, starring Gregory Kelly, capitalized on the play's contemporary success. By 1934, when the second film version was released, the material seemed dated: "This particular variation of the success story hasn't seemed quite so amusing since 1929," wrote Richard Watts; and he also felt that Spencer Tracy was a too-sentimentalized show-off—"too sympathetic and dashing. Mr. Tracy is so likable from the start that the exposure of his underlying pathos comes neither as a surprise nor as a dramatic climax." Moreover, the play's rich atmosphere and sense of place were diluted: "Where once Aubrey Piper lived and breathed in a definite environment he now moves about merely against a series of motion picture sets and locations."[54]

In 1947, Metro-Goldwyn-Mayer remade the film as a vehicle for Red Skelton, whose performance was generally considered more fully rounded than Tracy's and closer in spirit to Kelly's original. A. H. Weiler in *The New York Times* observed that "Skelton . . . is surprisingly natural and funny . . . he shows few evidences of the facial gymnastics to which he is heir."[55] The *Herald Tribune* reviewer noted that Skelton even hints "of adaptability to a tragic situation."[56]

The Show-Off missed the Pulitzer Prize by a very slim margin; when *Craig's Wife* received the award the following year, it was generally felt to be a consolation award. As reflections of American life, both plays are equally trenchant; and Kelly deserved the Prize for both.

III   Craig's Wife

Kelly created in Harriet Craig his second classic American archetype. Though the kind of character that Mrs. Craig so vividly incarnates was not, even at the time, an original creation, Kelly's was the most fully realized presentation of a type; and playgoers in 1925 felt they were seeing something new even if they weren't.[57] Indeed, Craig's wife, like "the show-off," "has . . . passed into the language. Her name, like Babbitt's, has become a byword. Inasmuch as it brands a whole genus, it affords a conversational shortcut."[58] Craig's wife is "a synonym for a variety of unlovely woman";[59] "a woman whom every playgoer will recognize with something like a start "[60] as the American Ice Maiden—an emasculating, willful, dominating American female.[61]

Kelly "found" her in exactly the same way he discovered all of his characters—from his observations of life. "Everybody knows several Mrs. Craigs," Kelly said in an interview shortly after the play opened. "I've seen hundreds of them. The woman in the play is a composite." Generalizing extravagantly, Kelly remarked that his Mrs. Craig is

the modern woman. She is less than the truth as I have seen it many times. People always refuse to believe in the theater the reality as they hear and see it in their everyday lives. . . . Woman has gone outside the home, found that she has been living in a world of romantic illusion about men, and is now thinking consciously about marriage as a means of insuring the modern more or less luxurious equivalent of food, shelter, and clothes. . . . She happened to fail because an unusual situation arises to reveal her to her husband. But for one who fails there are thousands who succeed. Sometimes it is a good thing for their husbands. They hold them to the line. Sometimes they ruin their husbands.[62]

Based on Kelly's own observations and kneaded into dramatic shape by his own antipathies, Craig's wife is the kind of heroine an audience loves to hate—and Kelly lets his spectators hate her for all she's worth. Kelly has said that he was warned that audiences, particularly women, wouldn't go to see an unflattering portrait; but this assumption was decisively disproved by the success of his play. "*Craig's Wife*," said Kelly, "proved that you don't need love in order to sell tickets."[63] Kelly did feel, however, that when Harriet is abandoned at the end of the play and stands dazed, absently allowing rose petals on her precious floor, she is a "pathetic figure. Audiences sighed."[64]

Until Mrs. Craig's final defeat, Kelly pursues his heroine relentlessly. She is a destructive, selfish woman, and she must be punished; Kelly desires his audience to share his zealous disapproval of her, and he wants it to enjoy his punishment of her. Despite the playwright's ferocious treatment of Harriet, the play is, however, an audience-pleaser because it is a superior melodrama. Its "popular" quality can be gauged by its tidy and efficient plot; and it is, in fact, the only plot play in the Kelly canon. In a most un-Kelly fashion, the plot is as boldly outlined as the character of Mrs. Craig. Tight, rigorous, clipped, "the entire action of the play transpires between 5:30 in the evening and 9 o'clock the next morning";[65] and the events that transpire are arranged to insure Mrs. Craig's ultimate isolation. The play's action neatly supports, therefore, a character's observation to Mrs. Craig: "People who live to themselves, Harriet, are generally left to themselves."

The play opens, typically, with the servants setting the scene; they alert the audience to the fact that Mrs. Craig is a demanding employer who will not tolerate a speck of dust morning, noon, or night. Mrs. Craig returns home after having visited her ailing sister with her niece Ethel. Because this niece is thinking of getting married, Mrs. Craig states her unromantic convictions about love and marriage: "the snare of romance,—that the later experience of life shows us to have been nothing more than the most impractical sentimentality. Only the majority of women are caught with the spell of it . . . and then they are obliged to revert right back to the almost primitive feminine dependence and subjection that they've been trying to emancipate themselves from for centuries. . . . I saw to it that my marriage should be a way toward emancipation for *me* . . . the independence of authority—*over* the man I married. . . . I married to be on my own."

In addition to this bald enunciation of Mrs. Craig's about marriage, Act I briskly suggests the routine of the Craig household. Harriet's vigilance is especially keen because, having just returned from a brief out-of-town visit, she is faced with setting the household machinery in motion once again. Snappily and authoritatively, she questions her servants; her niece; a helpless neighbor, Mrs. Frazier (a character whose love for her late husband emphasizes Harriet's love of things); her husband; and her husband's aunt, Miss Austen (who is wise to her and who tries to force the issue by alerting Mr. Craig to Mrs. Craig's true nature). Kelly beautifully manages his first act; the characters are all as sharply defined as the atmosphere of the house that Harriet runs with such pitiless rigor.

Were it not for introducing the plot complications, Act I would be in itself a fine character study.[66] In the opening moments, however, Mazie, the maid, conveniently remarks to Mrs. Harold, the head housekeeper, that there has been a local murder: "It says here they [the Passmores] were both found dead this morning in their home on Willows Avenue." When, soon after, the audience learns that Walter Craig was at the Passmores playing cards the night before, the mystery story is fully underway. Act I concludes with a fine melodramatic flourish as Harriet, who has just read about the murder, clutches the newspaper to her heaving bosom. Act II, devoted to the unraveling of the Passmore murders, moves at as clipped and as trimmed a pace as the efficient Craig housekeeping. The plot moves forward by cross-questionings—the usual Kelly method—but in Act II these rapid-fire questions are not of the customary, disinterested variety ("Will you bring me a glass of water?"; "What train did you take?"); they are sternly purposeful, despite Mrs. Craig's increasingly evasive answers.

In Act I, when she was informed by Mrs. Harold that Craig had called the Passmore number (Levering 4300), Mrs. Craig called it herself in order to satisfy her curiosity. Her call was traced; in Act II, detectives arrive to question her about the circumstances of the call; Mrs. Craig is vague, protecting herself and at the same time implicating Walter. When Walter returns home, he cross-examines Harriet about the purpose of the detectives' visit; she gets rattled and gives herself away. "It isn't for me to determine the degree of your guilt or innocence," she says cold-bloodedly. "I'm not interested. . . . I'm interested only in the impression on the popular mind,—and the respect of the community we've got to live in."

Act II ends with the most theatrical flourish in Kelly's work:

Walter, beginning to see the truth about his wife, smashes a figurine which Harriet has enshrined on the mantelpiece like an altar and which she will not permit the servants to dust (she has a special brush that she alone uses). To add emphasis to Walter's rebellion, he also flicks cigar ashes on Harriet's cherished rug. This obvious dramatic moment never fails to elicit wild applause from audiences, and it works in the reading, too: the timing is right; the gesture is apt and in character.

Act III is designed to get everyone out of the house as quickly as possible. Maizie, Mrs. Harold, Miss Austen, Ethel (accompanied by her fiancé), and finally Walter pack their bags and leave Harriet in sole possession of her Holy Temple. After everyone has fled, she receives a telegram informing her of her sister's death; and her isolation is complete.

The Act I exposition, the Act II complication and climax, and the Act III resolution make *Craig's Wife* a well-made play "whose three acts," as Joseph Wood Krutch has indicated, "end respectively with a question mark, an exclamation point, and a period, according to the established formula."[67] Kelly's dialogue matches the precision of his construction; the play's diction is skillfully adjusted to social classes, and the long speeches are built with graceful periods: "a pared, rigid, inlaid, close-packed dialogue too exact to be true."[68] The masters speak in an exceedingly cold, almost ritualized, diction: "the thing must be susceptible of some sort of adjustment"; "there *is* a danger in propinquity"; "For you're fighting for the life of your manhood, Walter; and I cannot in conscience leave this house without at least turning on the light here." The glacial tone corresponds to Harriet Craig's glacial house. The servants, however, are allowed to speak with a flavorful earthiness reminiscent of Mrs. Fisher: "I told her right up; I said, 'I'll dust no tree for nobody. . . . She sez, 'You mean you refuse to dust it?'—'Yes, I sez, 'I refuse,' and, I sez, 'what's more, I'm goin' to stay refuse.'"

In working out the motivations for his characters, Kelly didn't heed his own advice: "The playwright mustn't be too explicit, mustn't move among the peasantry." As Gilbert Gabriel observed, "It is the evident duty of one and almost all of these characters to point out the moral of it long before the married twain come wrestling and tumbling to its brink."[69] Though Kelly felt it was necessary to "convict Harriet [with] . . . her own words," he also felt that her motivations must be referred to "obliquely."[70] But Harriet's statements to Ethel about the function of marriage are hardly oblique, and Kelly's explanation for Harriet's obsession with her house is certainly glib: Harriet's mother was cheated out of her home and husband by an overbearing rival, and for years Harriet and her mother did not have a house of their own. In Kelly's eagerness to communicate to his audience, he explains too much and too neatly.

During its out-of-town tryout, *Craig's Wife* was subtitled, variously, *A Drama of the Changing Social Order* and (even more ambitiously) *A Drama of the Changing Social and Economic Order*. The play is nothing of the kind; for, like all of Kelly's work, it is essentially a character study—only this time the character portraiture is surrounded by a more complicated plot. Kelly tries to give stature to his characters "by departing from the specific to the general"—by stepping aside, as George Jean Nathan noted, "to offer a blackboard lecture proving by statistics that there are thousands of persons in the world like his characters."[71]

But Kelly does not relate his characters to any broad socioeconomic movements; moreover, as in *The Show-Off* and *The Torch-Bearers*, he has not given his material the kind of social accent it might have received from a more extroverted, public-spirited playwright. As Brooks Atkinson correctly observed: "There is no cause for social alarm. . . all the matter of this play seems purely the substance of [Harriet's] character." Although Kelly had again written a play about a distinctly American character, "equipped with all the machinery of American life," neither his character nor his milieu typifies a particular place or period.[72] Mrs. Craig and her home seem suspended in a curiously timeless vacuum, immune to the pressures and concerns of the outside world.

As critics indicated, the claustrophobic single-mindedness with which Kelly pursues his erring housewife gives the play its idiosyncratic stamp: "Kelly seems more interested in punishing Harriet than in probing her motivation . . . What Mr. Kelly fails to show, at least to the extent he should, is that along with something naturally hateful in Mrs. Craig there is something deeply sick. . . . she is a dangerous neurotic."[7] Most critics appreciated the play for what it was, but they wanted it to be a deeper study of character and a more probing analysis of American values: "[Kelly] seems too much the moralist and not enough the psychologist or for that matter the sociologist. . . . She is partly the product of her upbringing (as Mr. Kelly indicates), partly of a whole social structure (as Mr. Kelly fails to suggest)."[74]

Like virtually all of Kelly's characters, Mrs. Craig is suspended in a "pre-Freudian-Jungian-Shavian-Marxian air."[75] Claustrophobic, indifferent to the inherent social dimensions of its subject, far too pat as a study of a neurotic, *Craig's Wife* is a supremely skillful theater piece, a box-office melodrama—no more, no less. And, for all its "sharpness as theater—perhaps largely because of it—the play seems a little remote and unventilated, lacking the clank and ambiguity and vibration of real life."[76]

Craig's Wife, then, is not many of the things it might have been. It is not, for instance, a problem play in the manner of Pinero or Henry Arthur Jones; it is not a Shavian social drama; though it has comic elements, it is too stern to be labeled comedy; and it is not probing enough to merit fully its author's designation of "drama." It certainly isn't tragedy (as a few zealous reviewers of the time tried to contend, adducing the play's "stark, stripped line of action, the passages in duologue, the quick give-and-take of short-breathed speech, the rigid exclusion of actual violence from the stage, the relentless unfolding of a fatal scheme"[77]); nor is it comic-strip buffoonery, as suggested by an unhappy reviewer who preferred to the austerity of *Craig's Wife* such alternate titles as "What the Dust-hunter Becomes," or "Let Him Put His Tootsies on the Table."[78]

Craig's Wife is a Broadway commodity that features a little mystery, a few grim laughs, and a stern, simplistic moral to husbands and to wives to beware and to repent. A typical Kelly blend of the commercial and the esoteric, this play is a middle-brow confection with sporadic high-brow intentions. The play has suggestions of Strindberg and Ibsen, though Kelly said he wasn't really familiar with either writer at the time; it was only afterwards that he realized he had written a *Doll's House* in reverse,[79] a play that calls for the liberation of the husband rather than of the wife.

Craig's Wife played for two years in New York, thereby enjoying the longest run of any Kelly play. Chrystal Herne played Harriet "as a stylish, educated, attractive woman," and, to Kelly, the performance "was a fashion show."[80] In the 1947 revival (also directed by Kelly in his last Broadway venture), Judith Evelyn stressed the character's neurotic elements and made her an altogether less sympathetic figure; indeed, Harriet seemed more of a monster than she had in 1925. This revival was the only time in his career that Kelly received adverse criticism for his direction, which resulted in a production that moved too fast and too erratically. Like *The Show-Off*, *Craig's Wife* (directed by Kelly) fared miserably in London, the cranky reviewer for *The Times* maintaining, "Frankly, I cannot understand why *The Silver Cord* succeeded. I suppose we cannot be bunked twice with the same accent."[81]

Craig's Wife has not become the summer-stock staple that *The Torch-Bearers* and *The Show-Off* have, but Tallulah Bankhead did tour the straw-hat circuit in it in 1960, and her performance must have been something to see. *Craig's Wife* has been the basis of three films, the first a 1928 silent movie with Irene Rich and Warner Baxter that was "pleasingly subdued."[82] In 1936, it served as a star showcase for Rosalind Russell; this version was directed by Dorothy Arzner. In 1950, considerably revised (only scattered nuggets of original Kelly remained), the play was transformed into a Joan Crawford vehicle called *Harriet Craig*. For both the 1936 and 1950 versions, the publicity stressed the melodramatic angles: "What was Harriet Craig's lie? What did her kiss really mean? Her neighbor knew! Her niece suspected! Her housekeeper told! Behind drawn curtains the town whispered about her . . . as she lived her life of sham in a house locked to the world!"[83]

CHAPTER 5

The Problem Plays

A FTER three successive hits (and the Pulitzer Prize for *Craig's Wife*), Kelly was clearly at the peak of his career; and a new play of his was as keenly anticipated as a new one by O'Neill. By 1926, Kelly had proven himself that rare combination of a writer's writer, a critic's writer, and an audience's writer. His work was so respected and so *enjoyed*, in fact, that, when the opening of his fourth full-length play, *Daisy Mayme*, coincided with Eva Le Gallienne's setting the corner-stone of the Civic Repertory Theater on 14th Street, all the newspaper critics "neglected" the ceremony in order to go to the Playhouse Theater to see Kelly's latest.[1]

Though it is certainly a writer's play and a critic's play too, *Daisy Mayme* is not an audience's play: it has far too much manner and too little matter for the average Broadway crowd. Although all three hit plays exhibited quirks and personal obsessions, *Daisy Mayme* is one of Kelly's most privately focused, airless plays; and it was followed by two other oddities. *Behold the Bridegroom* (1927) was quite unlike anything Kelly had attempted before, at least in its surface trappings: who, after all, could have expected from Kelly a tragedy about love set in a Philip Barry milieu? Though *Maggie the Magnificent* (1929) marked a return to more traditional Kelly territory, it too is a problem play; for its heroine is a cold, prudish young woman who proved unlikable to practically everyone except her author.

Daisy Mayme attacks those who let "the willing horse pull the load"; *Behold the Bridegroom* tells us that a rich young girl who has lived a fast life can never reform even if she earnestly wants to; *Maggie the Magnificent* suggests that learning how to order servants about in a Long Island mansion is a worthy antidote to having been reared in a common household. In these three peculiar plays, then, Kelly is absorbed by his personal predilections; and, in writing to please himself and to satisfy his own moral standards, Kelly lost touch with his audience.

I *Daisy Mayme*

Beautifully "orchestrated," *Daisy Mayme* is a quintessential Kelly play, which means not only that it is peculiar but that it falls into that lonely middle range of comedy-drama inhabited by virtually no other American playwright. The play is at once too subdued and leisurely, too much like life and yet curiously too much of the theater, to enjoy popular acceptance; and, on the other hand, it is not thematically weighty enough, verbally colored enough, formally flashy enough, to endear itself to an intellectual audience.

The culmination of a natural line of development from *The Show-Off* to *Craig's Wife*, *Daisy Mayme* is a re-positioning of themes, character types, and techniques from Kelly's two box-office bonanzas. Like *Craig's Wife*, *Daisy Mayme* is a play about a house—in fact, even more than in Kelly's preceding play, the house itself is the central "character." The people in the play are obsessed by the house: "This house is nearly a hundred years old"; "I love an old-fashioned house"; "I love this house; and I've always loved it: and it would just about break my heart to see some strange woman come into it; especially one that wasn't worthy of it"; "There's something set and sensible-looking to me about an old-fashioned house. It looks as though it's been in the business of living a long time"; "I like this room best . . . this room's my idea of a good time. I think if I were dying and they let me sit in this room for fifteen minutes, I'd come to again"; " . . . she loves this house. She says when she hears the rain on those trees outside her window upstairs, she says she wants to pass right out of the picture."[2]

The chief antagonists for possession of the house are the owner's sister, Laura Fenner, and his potential wife, Daisy Mayme. Mrs. Fenner wants the house now that her sister Lydy has died, and she regards Daisy's friendly visit as a threat to her goal. All of the characters have a deep-seated attachment to the house: Cliff loves it because it is his mother's house; Mrs. Fenner wants to take possession of it because she feels she has been cheated out of a house of her own since her "delicate" husband never earned enough money to enable them to buy one; and Daisy is attracted to the house because it is old-fashioned and because, living in two rooms above a store, she too does not have her own dwelling.

The theme of "the house" is sounded just as urgently among the secondary characters: Laura's daughter Ruth, who is about to be married, wants as much as her mother to own her own house. "Ruth has a little; and she'd like to put it down on a house," Mrs. Fenner explains to Cliff. "She says she cannot see the sense of paying rent all your life and having nothing at the finish." Like her acquisitive mother, Ruth wants to wheedle a house from Cliff; for, in addition to owning such a big, comfortable, hotly contested house, he is a contractor who has built a row of nice, sturdy houses—ones that he does not intend to give away to his unlikable niece and her irresponsible husband-to-be: "I don't know why *I* should be expected to hand out houses to everybody that wants them."

Like Harriet Craig (and like Mrs. Fisher too, for that matter), the characters in *Daisy Mayme* regard ownership of a house as certain security: owning a house (or at least being firmly established in the house of someone else) means protection and permanence. No one in *Daisy Mayme* is nearly so nasty as Harriet Craig, but all of these people are as house-proud and as house-oriented as she is. Ownership of a house is, in fact, the deepest urge in all the characters; and it pushes them into a contest that has the impact of a struggle for basic survival. The contest is waged by subtle means—the raising or lowering of a window shade, the closing and opening of a piano, stealthy looks, pertinent glances, furtive gestures, sly verbal insinuations; but, despite the subtlety of the combat, the characters are engaged in a deadly duel.

There are actually four houses that figure prominently in the play and in the characters' thoughts: Cliff's womb-like, solid, tree-shaded, one-hundred-year-old house; Laura's rented house, which everyone hates, and which, because of its distastefulness, is really the principal catalyst, igniting the schemes of Laura and Ruth; Cliff's new, desirable, sturdy tract house; and Daisy's grim rented rooms. (Olly, Cliff's likable second sister, also, presumably, has a house; her "humor," however, is not her house, but her aches and pains which are concentrated in her troublesome left foot.)

Linked closely to the theme of the possession of houses in the design of the play is the familiar Kelly theme of *earning* the right of possession. Typically, Kelly's characters are subjected to the closest moral scrutiny; and we learn that Laura Fenner doesn't deserve her own house not only because she is petty and mean-spirited but also because she doesn't make her own way—she's one of those women who live off their men. Ruth and Charlie do not deserve their own house because Ruth has inherited her mother's smallness and selfishness and because Charlie is a parasite and a drifter, an Aubrey Piper gone completely sour. Kelly is highly critical of Charlie and Ruth, just as in *The Show-Off* and in *Craig's Wife* he cautions young couples against entering a marriage with romantic illusions and no money. Daisy Mayme alone deserves her own house; she is a woman who knows how to make her own way.

Character types, as well as themes, are a Kelly pastiche. With her horse laugh and her bubbling spirits, Daisy Mayme certainly resembles the show-off; Mrs. Fenner's meanness and her heightened awareness of public appearance are a variation of Harriet Craig; and Cliff, who always bears the family burdens because he is "the willing horse who pulls the load," resembles Mrs. Fisher and Walter Craig. And, like Walter Craig, Cliff is a good-natured man who is exploited by his ill-natured relatives and who is not very bright; he needs others to indicate to him that his house is not in order.

To certify their importance as well as their familiarity, Kelly relies upon his usual method of stressing the typicality of characters and situations. His characters, in fact, define each other as types; for example, Mrs. Fenner says that Daisy's "type" ". . . has no more home, Olly, than a tomcat. Couldn't you tell that by looking at her? . . . You heard her call him Cliff, didn't you?—and she's known him about four days. . . . That's the kind she is—doesn't lose any time. You know, the woods are full of women like her." And Daisy defines Laura's type, but she is honest enough to tell Laura directly what she thinks of her:

Daisy: Now, do you think it's necessary, Laura, for you to tell me what *your* name is. . . . I know it better than I know my own.
Mrs. Fenner: Well, then, I wish you'd use it, if you do.
Daisy: I might do more than that for you, Laura, if you're dumb enough to drive me to it. I'll spell your name out for you here sometime—backwards; and right in front of your brother too.

Cliff says of Charlie: "He's one of those drifter boys—that's going to get it easy at somebody else's expense."

The title character, however, is less a type than the others; for, although Daisy embodies various Kelly character traits, the combination of ingredients is unique in the canon. Like Aubrey, she is an optimist who brings laughter and fresh air to a house much in need of both; unlike Aubrey, though, she is not silly but is instead a responsible businesswoman. Daisy is not a gentlewoman, however, and Kelly's mostly favorable attitude toward her is therefore brushed with disapproval. Daisy is too noisy for Kelly's genteel predilections, and his appreciation of her is qualified: he likes her about as well as he likes any of his characters, but from a suitable distance. Brooks Atkinson has offered a balanced appraisal of her character: " . . . although Daisy turns out to be an agreeable sort in the end . . . she can be quite as disagreeable as her opponents. She settles down in this new house too easily . . . she is much too familiar . . . [with her] boisterous assurance and irritating good nature."[3] Arthur Hobson Quinn found her rather "too blatant and breezy,"[4] and Gilbert W. Gabriel noted that she has "the manners of a virtuous daughter of the regiment. . . . she roars and melts, chortles, slaps back. . . . "[5]

Considered as a comic character, Daisy is decidedly a pallid echo of Aubrey Piper. Charles Brackett, writing in *The New Yorker*, nicely qualified Daisy's limitations as a source of comedy: "*Daisy Mayme* is more like Mr. Kelly's *Show-Off* than his *Craig's Wife*, but to me it is not quite so successful simply because Daisy Mayme, the kind, canny, ordinary little woman who is its central character, is not as good theatrical material as was the show-off himself. One always laughed at Aubrey; one seldom laughs at Daisy Mayme. She is too likable. Nor does one laugh *with* her, for while she is considered 'a scream' by her friends, as a humorist she is merely exactly as funny as a small town life-of-the-party is apt to be."[6] That Daisy does not amuse as fully as Aubrey Piper, however, is deliberate; the reduced amount of laughter suits the play's quiet tone. *Daisy Mayme* maintains a secure balance between the robust chuckles of *The Show-Off* and the high-strung squabbles of *Craig's Wife*.

Daisy Mayme, in fact, is Kelly's most sustained achievement. There are neither tonal miscalculations nor moralistic intrusions. The play is happily free of Act III lectures (*The Torch-Bearers*); of audience-pleasing last-minute reversals of fortune (*The Show-Off*); and of stock, well-made play contrivances (*Craig's Wife*). *Daisy Mayme* lives and breathes entirely in the realm of Realism, and the critics lavishly praised the play's unblemished Realistic texture. Stark Young, for example, praised the homely American diction: "In a field that is indeed everyday, domestic, homely and American, we hear from the first curtain our English language take on its infectious beat and beloved familiar savor. . . . Mr. Kelly has a gift of diction that is far ahead of anyone in the American thea-ter. . . . *Daisy Mayme* exhibits the perfection of domestic, biting speech converted into theater."[7] Alexander Woollcott commented upon its Realism: "I know no writer for the American stage who can so get the smell of everyday life into his plays."[8] And Percy Ham-mond observed that "No dictaphone could have been more accurate in reporting the details of a fortnight in an average American house-hold."[9]

The play's quiet, steady, entirely unbroken theatrical naturalism, however, prompted some critics to want something showier. Stark Young felt that "what we need is what we shall have to call after all something in the line of the traditional comic surprise, something by which the knots are drawn closer toward the end and the uncer-tainty of the happy ending hazarded. . . . "[10] The play's relentless miniature-portrait method worked against itself, according to Gil-bert Gabriel: "Mr. Kelly has confronted his footlights with persons who look, speak and think in pitilessly lifelike ways. The stage takes inevitable revenge. It turns their play quite lifeless. . . . With that amazing knack he has of presenting [his characters] in most human terms, Mr. Kelly manages to make them all the more inhu-man."[11]

More than any other Kelly play, *Daisy Mayme* elicited compari-sons with Chekhov. Casually structured, a subtle mixture of seem-ingly "dictaphonic" dialogue and theatrical heightening, Kelly's play, like those of Chekhov, is filled with ordinary, second-rate characters; and its seemingly snapshot view of a particular social class is satire blended with sympathy, objective reporting laced with subjective coloring. Kelly's canvas, obviously, is much more re-stricted than Chekhov's; for no large social or historical forces oper-ate behind the play's facade. Kelly's characters, unlike Chekhov's, are neither visionaries nor idealists—they simply want houses of their own to live in. Kelly's tone is acrid, dry, sardonic—much more limited, of course, than Chekhov's. But, in its feeling for real life, in its quiet blending of the natural and the theatrical, and in its unhur-ried pace and uncluttered structure, the play does share common elements with the work of Chekhov, just as *Craig's Wife* shares with Ibsen's plays a critical examination of an unhealthy marriage and a belief in the necessity for self-knowledge.

Deliberately avoiding the broader frameworks of the plays of

Ibsen or Chekhov, Kelly confines himself in *Daisy Mayme* (as throughout his work) to the domestic feud; and no one is better than Kelly at suggesting petty grievances and small dissatisfactions—the aches and pains of making supper, of cleaning house, of worrying about overcoats and rubbers, of speculating about the weather, and of complaining about the neighbors. *Daisy Mayme* achieves its sense of unity through Kelly's evident delight in having his characters tell each other off. "I do not know Mr. Kelly," wrote Charles Brackett, "but I picture him as a rather mild gentleman given to savage, secret indignations and fond of muttering to himself long speeches in which he recites to the object of those indignations the exact appraisal of their meanness."[12]

The brittle retorts that comprise the following exchange between Laura and Olly are an accurate gauge of the Kelly tone (his special brand of dry humor) and subject matter (very small events indeed):

Olly: Well, I'm here, aren't I, and that's all you are, Laura.
Laura: I know, Olly, but I've *been* here since ten o'clock this morning; and going every minute of the time since. And I don't think it would have hurt you at all to come over here today and give a hand.
Olly: It *wouldn't* have hurt me at all; and I should have come over willingly if I'd known they were coming home to-day.
Laura: You knew as much about it as I did.
Olly: Well, I wouldn't preen myself so much on it, Laura, if I were you.
Laura: I'm not preening myself at all.
Olly: You know it's very lately that you've become so industrious around this house.
Laura: I've always been as industrious as you've been, I think.
Olly: You know how industrious you've been, Laura. But, don't be alarmed,—I won't take any of the credit for your work when Cliff comes.
Laura: Oh, I knew you'd turn it that way.
Olly:That's what's the matter with you, Laura, I know all your tricks. . . . You're furious that I got here at all. For if you were so very anxious to have me here, you could have called me up.
Laura: A lot of good that would have done me; you've never been in once yet to my knowledge when I *have* called.
Olly: Well, if I haven't been in I've been out. I knew the minute you'd see this new suit and hat on me you'd start *something*. . . .
Laura: I didn't know your suit and hat *were* new.
Olly: Don't tell lies, dear.
Laura: How should I know?
Olly: You knew, all right. . . . You know it if I get a new handkerchief; and it's like a red rag to you.

Laura: You get so many new things I can't keep track of them.
Olly: Well, if I do they're paid for. And I wouldn't get them if I didn't need them.
Laura: I don't know why you needed another black suit when you got one only a month ago for the funeral.
Olly: That coat is too short. It makes me look too squat. It has absolutely no line from the shoulder to the hip; and I'm too dumpy. That is the one line I must have; and if I don't have it, I might just as well be sitting down.

This dialogue indicates the spirit of the play—the tart exchanges; the eternal fussings and fumings over small personal concerns. It's not a profound play, certainly, but within the modest limits it sets for itself, it is incisive and accurate.

The play is enlivened by the entrance of Mr. Filoon, the non-agenarian neighbor of the Mettingers. His part is conceived as a vaudeville "turn."[13] Filoon has no real business in the play other than to interrupt the Mettingers' squabblings; and he is obviously introduced for change of pace and for subsidiary coloring. Crusty and spry, liberatingly tactless, he underlines the play's wry flavor at the same time that he interjects a fresh rustic quality of his own:

Filoon: . . . No, Ma'm, I lived in the city of Lancaster. . . .That's where I was first married. In the year eighteen and sixty-seven. Two years after the War of the Rebellion. Fifty-nine years ago. I was turned thirty-two years of age. And if I live till the twenty-eighth day of this coming August, I'll be ninety-one.
Daisy: And do you feel pretty well as a rule, Mr. Filoon?
Filoon: Wha' say?
Daisy: I say, do you get pretty good health, as a rule?
Filoon: All but the legs.
Cliff: Do your legs bother you, Mr. Filoon?
Filoon: Won't carry me nowhere. All shot to Hell.
Cliff: That's too bad.
Filoon: Yes, that's where it shows, in the legs. But outside of that,—I'm as good as ever.
Cliff: Well, that's fine.
Filoon: Yes, fit as a fiddle. Eat anything at all and sleep eight hours out of the twenty-four.
Cliff: You're a wonder, Mr. Filoon.
Filoon: That's right; there ain't a many like me.

The play's squabbling is also relieved by the ending, a singularly unromantic, down-to-earth, folksy proposal of marriage in which

Daisy Mayme finally gets her man. Daisy's final speech is about as close to conventional sentiment as Kelly ever got: " . . . I've always thought I'd *like* to be married—to some steady man—that smoked good cigars— and live in an old-fashioned house—with trees around it—and just sit there in the evening and listen to some doll of a daughter play the piano—while I made dresses for her." At the end, Cliff's daughter May plays the piano, Daisy sits in the lady's chair ("I've always wanted to *be* a lady"), Cliff "blows a long line of smoke towards her"—and all is pure romance. This ending is the happiest and most "popular" one of any Kelly play; and, unlike the twist at the end of *The Show-Off*, the happy ending develops naturally from character and situation—it has been earned.

II Behold the Bridegroom

Before the New York opening of *Behold the Bridegroom*, Kelly announced to the press that he was going "to take a long rest." From the premiere in 1922 of *The Torch-Bearers* until the December, 1927, opening of *Behold the Bridegroom*, Kelly had been working steadily, casting and directing on Broadway and in London and going on tour with his plays. Intimately involved in every phase of every production, Kelly had certainly earned a vacation; but his announcement of an interruption in his writing was prompted by motives other than the need for a rest. At the time, Kelly regarded *Behold the Bridegroom* as his most important achievement; he had always thought of himself as a serious writer; and the high seriousness of his current play reinforced his conviction of the theater's moral and educational function (Kelly was especially proud of the fact that *Behold the Bridegroom* was frequently "used in the pulpit").[14]

Kelly said he was going to take it easy for a while in order to write a play equal in stature to this new one: "Mr. Kelly said he would never write any more plays just to entertain theatergoers. . . . Perhaps if he writes any more plays he will aim to be a modern Ibsen."[15] But, in announcing his temporary withdrawal from the theater, Kelly may well have been anticipating the play's financial failure. A *succès d'estime*, *Behold the Bridegroom* ran for only eighty-eight performances; and the play's inability to find an audience convinced Kelly that his type of play could not be produced on Broadway.

Containing as *Behold the Bridegroom* does the moralistic fervor of all of his previous work, this play does not represent the divergence that many reviewers of the time noted with surprise. But the play does represent departures of sorts; for, unlike Kelly's earlier works, the play is set not among the middle class (or the lower middle class) but in high society. Unlike his other plays, in which tragic implications are merely peripheral, *Behold the Bridegroom* is conceived entirely as tragedy, and it is Kelly's sole attempt in the genre. Despite its dry, modern touch, the play is tragedy in much the same spirit as Dumas *fils*, Pinero, and Henry Arthur Jones. For Kelly has based his drama on the traditional story of the erring woman of the world—"a hussy of the high world," he calls her[16]—who must pay for her past sins.

Antoinette Lyle, the spoiled daughter of a prodigally wealthy New York businessman, has lived fast and free; she lived with Lennie Rooks "for four months at San Sebastian the summer before last," she had caused Harvey Price to separate from his wife, and she had paid the wife a hundred thousand dollars to maintain silence. Tony's frank cousin, Eleanor Ridgeway, tells her: "I think life is beginning to play out with you. You've *been* everywhere, you've *seen* everything, and you've *had* everything. And it isn't enough,— for *your particular* kind of nature."

Tony has become bored and restless, but (and here's the play) she is given a reprieve when she meets Spencer Train, a handsome, noble young man. Tony realizes, however, that her past life has made her unfit for a man like Train: "Mr. Train is a good man; and what have *I* left to give him?" A foolish "virgin," she mourns: "My lamp was not trimmed and burning when the cry was raised; and so I mustn't whine if I am not permitted to go into the marriage supper."

The play is constructed around the Puritan sense of justice in which "the damned must be given one glimpse of paradise before they are plunged into hell forever."[17] Tony is allowed, therefore, a vision of what her life might have been if her past had qualified her for Train. Since Kelly maintained that he wrote the play as a demonstration of "the inevitability of the returning tide,"[18] Tony cannot escape the moral stain of her past indecencies. Self-convicted, she repines; and she expires.

A dying courtesan, too late repentant; a hero who wears a white rose in his lapel; a distraught suitor who kills himself when the courtesan firmly rejects him—these are the flatly conventional theatrical materials from which Kelly builds his play. But, if the play does not reach the tragic heights that Kelly clearly intended, neither does it descend to the level of melodramatic bathos that a bald summary of its elements might suggest. For Kelly has protected himself against the inherent sentimentality of his concept both by his distinctly unsentimental dialogue, and by his passionate conviction.

Kelly has countered the "romantically sentimental" elements with his "hard-polished, swift playwriting"; he never once allows the audience to "mop its eyes."[19] For a play which, after all, concerns "an overpowering emotion and its consequences,"[20] *Behold the Bridegroom* is a remarkably level-headed play. Tony Lyle is not given to emotional outbursts; rather, much like the characters in *Craig's Wife*, she discusses her "condition" in elegantly constructed periods and with a decorum befitting her elevated social position—an attention to decorum that gives the play something of the air of moving among "our betters" and that indicates Kelly is not so comfortable as a playwright with the "400" characters as with the Fishers, the Mettingers, and the Craigs.[21]

Kelly works against melodrama not only in creating an altogether clear-sighted and unfailingly well-spoken heroine but also in allowing the other characters to discuss Tony's condition with clinical precision and detachment. This "discussion" quality is particularly apparent in the beginning of Act III, in which the two doctors present to Tony's father the conclusions of their diagnoses. A dry scene indeed, its dead-pan earnestness borders dangerously on the ludicrous; but the scene does avoid sentimentality. Kelly's doctors have that tendency for generalization that afflicts many Kelly characters: "Years ago they [cases like this] were not at all uncommon—especially among women. They used to be known in those days as cases of repining,—lack of the will to live. But they've become rather rare these late years: due, I have no doubt, to the many compensating factors in modern life—people are not apt to take any one experience too seriously."

Kelly's attempts to psychoanalyze Tony are as elementary as his providing Harriet Craig with a weak mother who didn't know how to keep her husband or her house. In both cases, the effort to explain his heroines is much too oversimplified; and seemingly, "Mr. Kelly has never forgotten the lesson of his vaudevillian days, that a point, to be driven home to an audience, must be three times hammered."[22] Kelly's account of psychosomatic illness is especially obvious and dated; for his Doctor Loebell says, "We've probably been hugging certain of our present theories too closely. . . . Particularly, the theory that the physical condition is simply the chorus of its atoms. . . . I assure you there are more things in the woman heart than are dreamed of in Materia Medica." Kelly's enlistment of psychiatry is used not only to explain his heroine but to modernize his theme. He introduces "modern science" in order to enforce the point that women still die of unrequited love—even in 1927.

Some of the reviewers felt Kelly's "high" theme needed more elevated language; when Tony "beholds the mystery" at the end of Act I, does the play "need verse, not pantomime?"[23] Kelly meets the seriousness of his theme in the only way that he can—not by being poetic and high-toned (he is not, thank goodness, Maxwell Anderson), but by writing in a pared-down, formal, elegant style. His greatest reaching for the poetic is in some of the heightened, archaic syntax: "I have seen the man, at whose bidding I might rise to the fulfillment of any worth that's in me." The fancy-sounding title comes from the twenty-fifth chapter of Matthew, the parable of the foolish virgins; and the dialogue does, at times, aim for a kind of biblical incantation; but it is heightened, rhythmical *prose* rather than poetry.[24]

Kelly departs from the predominant highly modulated tone in the finale,[25] in which there is real emotion. He allows his heroine a colorful if conventional death scene, but he avoids cliché at the end: "At this instant—the young woman having been carried out unconscious—there is a tragic pause, and you expect that, after a second or two, the nurse or father will appear at the rear door, murmur sententiously with bowed head, followed by a slow curtain. But here, as throughout the play, Mr. Kelly gets away from stencils."[26] At the very end, Kelly supplies another twist—the kind of unconvincing reversal such as he used for *The Show-Off*. Train wonders if perhaps *he* was not ready for what Tony had to offer; and, coming from the priggish Train, this "retraction" can be explained only by the character's temporary shock. But, in allowing Train to have second thoughts about Tony and in avoiding the conventional announcement of death, Kelly has tried hard to refresh his ending; and, if Train's character lacks conviction, Kelly has at least skirted the charge of staleness. He has, however, yielded to cliché for his conclusions to the first two acts: at the end of Act I, a transfixed Tony stares into the middle distance at "the miracle" of the bridegroom; and, at the end of Act II, Tony falls in a dead faint after she hears that the man who wanted to marry her, and whom she has rejected, has committed suicide.

The play's mixture of convention and variation is typical of Kelly, who always accepted the limitations of the theater, "making them and his design mutually elastic. As usual, he avoids no familiar means of the stage, if that means, at the given moment, suits his purpose."[27] Until its stock conclusion, his Act I is a fresh beginning for a play on the repentant courtesan theme. Set in an elegant conservatory on a lovely summer afternoon, Act I is bright and snappy; and Kelly introduces a comic socialite, Connie Peyton, who hasn't the remotest connection to plot but whose aimless, pert gossip supplies colorful social context. The clipped accents of the Act I prattle and its *bon ton* suggest Philip Barry.

But even when the play goes sour, or when it isn't deep enough, it has stature; and it is held in place by Kelly's moral austerity. He is as avid about castigating Antoinette Lyle and the type she represents as he is about Harriet Craig and her type. Kelly has no use for either kind of woman—except insofar as they afford examples for moral reformation. However, Kelly likes Tony Lyle much more than he likes Harriet Craig, and he wants the audience to be impressed by Tony's self-awareness—her keen recognition of her errors as much as anything qualifies her for tragic honors. Despite his respect for Tony's honesty, though, Kelly, unflinching disciplinarian that he is, finally disapproves of her. He expresses his final attitude through the unintentionally prudish Spencer Train: "I think the kind of life that girls in your daughter's set are permitted to live rather tends to make that sophistication very real. . . It's the *nature* of the gossip that I am concerned with chiefly, Mr. Lyle; and whether it's founded or unfounded, it implies an idea of—personal liberty—that I should be rather fearful about including in my—private life." This self-righteousness recalls Harriet Craig, but Kelly is not now mocking the sentiments. That the playwright thought he was creating a likable hero in Train is another of his miscalculations: Spencer Train is simply not human enough to make the audience believe that the heroine is so strongly attracted to him.

Tony is an intelligent girl; and, though she is now willing to reform, she shares her creator's conviction that there can be no forgiveness for her past life. Like the author, Tony believes she cannot escape the moral and psychic damage of having been "a hussy of the high world." This response to Tony's past is stodgy, but there can be no mistaking Kelly's absolute sincerity. Joseph Wood Krutch wrote a beautifully cogent analysis of Kelly's Puritanism:

[Kelly] is, though not in any debased sense of the word, a puritan, and a puritan wishes to understand all, not in order that he may pardon all, but in order that he may know how all may be adequately punished. . . . I can respect the moral sincerity which has enabled him to develop an almost pietistic thesis without falling into mere priggishness on the one hand or into rant on the other, but I honestly doubt that nature is constructed upon any plan so in accord with a puritan sense of moral fitness. . . . Artists and moralists both love to contemplate the irreparable . . . but nature is more compliant. Time cannot be called back and what has been physically destroyed cannot be found again, but nothing else is irretrievably lost and there are no sins that ought not and cannot be forgiven, for we are not made of stuff so stern as the puritan conscience would wish.[28]

Behold the Bridegroom is, therefore, the most uncompromising play in the canon; and Kelly wrote it to satisfy his own stern moral convictions rather than to appease popular sentiment. Kelly so disapproves of Antoinette Lyle and treats her so harshly that audiences end pitying the forlorn woman. Kelly, who likes Tony in spite of himself, makes her capacity for moral reform so evident that we can only rebel at his severe decision to have her die. Since the punishment exceeds the crime, we respond to the play contrary to the author's intentions: we like Tony; we do not like Spencer Train. In fact, we approve of Tony; we believe she has seen her past in all its empty folly and is now prepared and able to transcend it. This difference in response between Kelly and his audience cost him the popular success he had enjoyed with *The Torch-Bearers*, *The Show-Off*, and *Craig's Wife*. But writing to express his own moral values, unpopular as they may be, was clearly more important to Kelly than writing for "the gigglers."

III   Maggie the Magnificent

Maggie the Magnificent lasted only thirty-two performances; and, unlike *Behold the Bridegroom*, it was not a *succès d'estime*. Written according to the same exacting morality found in the preceding play, *Maggie* is even less an audience show. In an interview Kelly held after the largely unfavorable notices were in, he remarked that "Broadway is not in a mood to appreciate plays that are written without concession to the mood of the moment." To him, audiences were "led astray by the fact that he was absorbed with the mental processes of his characters without leading them into the violent situations to which Broadway" had become accustomed. "The absence of rape, murder, and arson is," he felt, "resented, because these narcotics have been fed to first-nighters now for many, many weeks."[29]

In another post-mortem interview, Kelly told Brooks Atkinson: "In the present era . . . a playwright must choose between amusing the gigglers and writing what he feels to be true." Atkinson concludes that Kelly's dedication to the truth as he sees it has carried him "into the realm of the unpleasant and unpopular. . . . From *The Torch-Bearers* to *Maggie the Magnificent* [is to go] from sure-fire nonsense to grim, uncompromising truth." Atkinson's evaluation is exaggerated since *The Torch-Bearers* has an underlying sobriety that protects it from designations of farce or burlesque; and *Maggie* contains compromises, especially in the blurred conclusion. But the general direction of Kelly's development is clear enough; for, as Atkinson correctly notes, Kelly "has steadily refused to capitalize his theatrical assets."[30]

Other critics were less kind about Kelly's increasing seriousness. The anonymous critic for *Judge* wrote that "George Kelly, like the clown who would play Hamlet, aspires to write Ibsen. Possessing a gift for low humor that should be sufficient unto his pride he somewhat ashamedly puts it behind him, wipes the flour from his face, takes off his cardboard red nose and his pantaloon costume and, making himself up in Norwegian whiskers, hopes to trick us into the impression that he is a very profound, serious and even mordacious fellow"[31] And Arthur Pollock in the *Brooklyn Eagle* observed that "Kelly tries to make each new play better than its predecessors, and in doing so he has the air of a playwright forcing his growth. He cannot forget himself or what is expected of him and sit down simply and have his fling. He must get to the bottom of things. But he is unable to reach the bottom. His place is on the surface. . . . [he is] a keen observer, and [he] creates a picture of that surface alone."[32]

Critical concensus was, therefore, that Kelly was misjudging his talents and was mistakenly aspiring toward "deep" drama when his true gifts were as a mimic, a cartoonist, a *farceur*—designations anathematic to Kelly himself. Critics always regarded Kelly as a leading American playwright; they always respected his work even if they did not enjoy it: but they were particularly impatient with *Maggie;* and they scolded Kelly for alienating himself from audiences who had enjoyed *The Torch-Bearers, The Show-Off,* and *Craig's Wife.*

In *Behold the Bridegroom,* Tony Lyle recalls the visit of a prim, efficient secretary who had come to check her undistributed income. Tony, who had been dancing until six o'clock in the morning, had had difficulty in preparing herself for the late afternoon meeting with a secretary who had probably been crisp and businesslike since the break of dawn. Tony respects the secretary; so, obviously, does Kelly, since he has used her prototype as the heroine of *Maggie the Magnificent.* The Maggie of the play, however, is alienating; dressed severely in black, she is all hard, sharp lines and deadly efficiency. As Joseph Wood Krutch observed, "She is neat, orderly, assured, competent, and correct, but only Mr. Kelly could admire her with warmth. . . . We are expected to feel in her an austere nobility, but what we actually feel is only a kind of spinsterish frigidity."[33] In brief, Kelly makes the same error he made in *Behold the Bridegroom* and in *Craig's Wife:* his audience likes the characters it is supposed to dislike, and it disapproves of the characters designed for its moral edification.

Like most of Kelly's plays, *Maggie the Magnificent* is about domestic squabbling; but the quarrelsome family now belongs to a lower-middle-class milieu reminiscent of the Fisher household in *The Show-Off,* though the tone of the arguments is closer to that of the wrangling sisters in *Daisy Mayme.*[34] The principal conflict in *Maggie* occurs between vulgarity and "class." Maggie's mother, Mrs. Reed, a tough little woman who had to get married, is resentful because her artist-husband always treated her with condescension. Maggie, who is as unlike her mother as she can be, aspires to "The Finer Things"; and the class war that has divided Maggie's parents is thus waged again between mother and daughter. Kelly said that he wanted to link this family feud to large social issues: "I had in mind a problem that is fundamental in our present social structure—the throwback in the family. There arises an antagonism between mother and daughter, between blood relatives, that is due to the intricate racial and social mixtures that have been going on for the last few generations. I studied a girl who strives beyond her mother's understanding."[35]

Maggie is not a drama about social forces, however, but a play of purely private focus about the consequences of misalliance, in which the playwright offers the undemocratic notion that the intermingling of classes is a dangerous affair. Maggie—to free herself from the contaminating environment of her common mother, her even commoner brother Elwood, and her commonest yet sister-in-law Etta—must leave; and, after her mother slaps her at the culmination of their most heated argument, she does so, going to a country estate entrusted to her management by her employer. Kelly is entirely in sympathy with Maggie's departure: "I showed the girl's rebellion because her mother had slapped her; her decision that only when the mother was at her mercy could she solve the problem."[36]

This vengeance theme is decidedly unpopular material. Richard Dana Skinner, writing in *Commonweal*, shrewdly noted: "In *The Show-Off*, everyone in the audience could detect himself and smile at the detection. In *Craig's Wife*, every woman in the audience could detect her neighbor—a slight but important distinction. But I doubt if there will be many mothers or daughters who will see themselves, or even their near neighbors, in Mrs. Reed and Maggie. Somehow the circumstances of their lives are too special to give them general value."[37]

Maggie the Magnificent, a generation-gap comedy, takes the side of the rebellious child—but the rebel is much more conservative than her antagonist. There is no triumph in Maggie's escape not only because what she is escaping to—a big, rich house—seems frivolous but also because, in the climactic Act II argument, the sympathy of the audience shifts from the younger Maggie to the mother. Kelly may well regard his Mrs. Maggie Reed as the personification of vulgarity, but his dramatic talents are more engaged in the creation of her character than they are in that of her self-righteous daughter. For all her boisterousness, spitefulness, and orneriness, Mrs. Reed is a vital, palpable character—one of the roundest in the Kelly canon—and Maggie seems bloodless in contrast. Stark Young provided a splendid appreciation of Kelly's portrait of Mrs. Reed:

. . . this woman, born common, married by her seducer, who despised her and shut the door on the rest of her family, hating him even in death and still hurt, dumbly and fiercely, after so many years, by the sting of his contempt. She sees the whole thing survive in this daughter whom she resents, is proud of, sends to school, baits and abuses and takes money from; she is frightened about her secret; she adores the worthless son, in whom her own blood comes out; and, finally, at the very last, she is saved, deserted, pitied, scorned by them all, but is always baffled, stupid, violent and hurt.[38]

Tight-lipped, severe, virtuous Maggie is no match for her flesh-and-blood mother. The real difference between them—the mother's common humanity; the daughter's austere morality—is under-scored in the climactic Act II leave-taking:

Mrs. Reed: Don't you think I have any heart?—that I want to see my own daughter walk out and leave her home.
Maggie: No,—I *don't* think you have any heart,—where I'm con-cerned. . . .
Mrs. Reed: That's a pretty hard thing for a girl to say to her Mother, Maggie.
Maggie: It's the truth:—so why shouldn't I say it. You and I have just been—*putting up* with each other all our lives; why should we go on doing it . . . We haven't one solitary thing in common: any more than many another Mother and daughter—that'd never even meet—only that they happen to *be* Mother and daughter. . . . (with a quiet, deadly emphasis) *You hit me.*
Mrs. Reed:—the only thing I can say is that—I'm sorry I done it. (She sinks into the chair, defeated) I *can't* do any more than that.
Maggie: I'm sorry you didn't do it long ago; for then I'd have left long ago. . . . It isn't right that a girl like me should be at the mercy of a woman like you. . . . You *hit* me. . . . *That's* how much you respect me. And the only way to keep you from ever—*daring*—to do such a thing again,—is to do what I'm doing now.[39]

This powerful scene works *against* the author's intentions in that Maggie seems narrow, stubborn, and unlikably proud; Mrs. Reed is forgiving, baffled, malleable, fully human, and sympathetic. In fact, an audience can only agree with her assessment of Maggie: "She's as *hard* as that piece of wood:—walkin' out and leavin' her own people, for the stranger, that wouldn't lose a night's rest if she was dyin'.— But, she'll get paid for it if she lives long enough—people always does. And then she'll know—what it is she's done to *me* this night."
Mrs. Reed's fullness as a character is in large part traceable to

Kelly's flavorful dialogue; she is fitted out in the best Kelly dictaphonic style. Maggie, in contrast, has no tangible dramatic voice; she's all correct grammar and stiff syntax—Kelly's almost inevitable style for his refined or upper-class characters. Moreover, Kelly's concept of character, and of morality, is eccentric. His standards here do not seem fully reasonable or even humane; for, as Joseph Wood Krutch indicates,

Hate seems to be the real source of his inspiration, and one is almost inclined to suspect that behind the harshness of his attitude lies some personal experience which would have to be known before one could entirely understand the vehemence of certain feelings which destroy the proportions of the work for the ordinary spectator. He likes certain persons and despises certain others with an abandon which seems not quite reasonable. He has idiosyncratic standards of judgment and he distributes rewards and punishments according to some personal canon of poetic justice which leaves the spectator less satisfied than vaguely resentful. . . . Mr. Kelly is not in tune with his audience and he does not succeed in making it in tune with him.[40]

In addition to these problems, Kelly devotes too much time to brother Elwood's marital difficulties, which are irrelevant to the central mother-daughter conflict except to validate the family's irrefutable commonness. Besides, Elwood and his wife Etta are like characters from another play: Etta is a flapper—cheap jewelry, bleached hair, tight red dresses; and Elwood, a tough little bootlegger. Both are amusing caricatures, and both surely derive their being from Kelly's vaudeville experience. But "Ibsen and vaudeville do not mix."[41] Kelly always had trouble adjusting levels of concept and intention: Etta and Elwood are there to entertain, their dilemma (Etta's infidelity) is treated lightly; but, in both their tone and their function, the characters do not fit in with the stern mother-daughter drama.

Kelly has also blurred the focus by providing a soft Act III, one which tries—too late—to win the audience by allowing universal reconciliations. Only the unrepentant, and presumably irredeemably common Etta, is excluded from the general good will; Elwood promises to reform—divorce from Etta, no more bootlegging, and an honest job as a chauffeur. And, at least tentatively, mother and daughter establish a truce. There is even a young man—Tom Ward—on hand to suggest the possibility of marriage for

Maggie. But their proposal scene is another of Kelly's cold, hard glances at marriage. Maggie is, of course, very practical about marriage: "I suppose it's that I'm afraid of the *sordidness* of life, Tom;— I've had so much of it. And it can come so insidiously in marriage."

But Kelly's most serious miscalculation is his attempt to make Maggie earn our respect by her competent management of the estate: "And when Ackerman comes back, Burnley, will you have him bring the big car at five,—we'll drive along the river before dinner." This altogether undemocratic assumption that the ability to command servants indicates some special competence and even nobility is hardly endearing. And yet clearly, as we watch Maggie descending the stairs, we are, like Mrs. Reed, to regard her "in silent wonderment."

Good individual moments exist in the play in the character of Mrs. Reed; in the first-act squabbles and establishment of the routine of the inveterately common Reed household; in the rhythmic Kelly dialogue; in the sardonic humor; and in the low comedy "humors" of the characters played by James Cagney and Joan Blondell. A richly Kelly play in both its strengths *and* its faults, the faults outweighed the strengths for Kelly himself; and he chose, unfortunately, not to publish the play: "I went wrong on it. I started to write one thing and wound up with another. . . . A playwright must never get off the track."[42]

CHAPTER 6

Two Plays about the Theater

KELLY'S four final contributions to the theater form two complementary pairs: *Philip Goes Forth* (1931) and *Reflected Glory* (1936) are plays about the theater; and they mark Kelly's first return to the subject since *The Torch-Bearers* in 1922; and *The Deep Mrs. Sykes* (1945) and *The Fatal Weakness* (1946) are Kelly's finest attacks on his favorite type, the suburban matron, and are the most eccentric work of an eccentric writer; as such, they represent something like a final flowering. The 1930's plays of the theater are unmistakable Kelly, but they are less specialized than the two final plays. The dramatist's usual techniques and touches are certainly in evidence—the compulsive absorption with cigarettes and vases of roses; the chatter about the time of day and the state of the weather; and the formalized greetings and leave-takings. Such business is as uncannily accurate as ever and also as droll and as dead pan. However, these two plays about the theater have more in common with conventional plays than most of Kelly's work.

Although these trimmings are delightful, the basic concepts of the two plays are disappointingly ordinary, for Kelly has written two standard theater stories: one about the country boy who goes to New York because he wants to make it in the theater; the other, about the actress torn between a career and private life. The working out of the fates of Philip Eldridge in *Philip Goes Forth* and of Muriel Flood in *Reflected Glory* are nonetheless marked by the playwright's austere and idiosyncratic morality. Therefore, despite their seeming conventionality, these two archetypal plays are yet personal enough in tone and point of view to qualify as authentic, if not strongly flavored, Kelly dramas.

Both plays are addressed to Kelly's concern with professional competence. Since in both cases the vocation in question is theater, the problem of competence is examined with particular scrutiny.

Both dramas express Kelly's reverence for the theater and even more for those who are theatrically gifted. For Kelly, true theatrical ability is equivalent to a state of grace; talent is not acquirable; and acting, writing, and directing are instinctive, God-given capabilities. These two plays are about the test of theatrical talent; Philip does not have it; Muriel Flood does; and everything else in the two dramas depends upon these indisputable facts.

I Philip Goes Forth

Always conscious of moral purpose, Kelly wrote *Philip Goes Forth* as a warning to potential playwrights that, if they are not innately gifted and wish to avoid disappointment, they should not clutter the theatrical marketplace but stay home and do the work they are best qualified to do. Kelly does not even entertain the notion that Philip's attempt and failure are good things in themselves since "getting it out of one's system" is merely a waste of time according to the severe Kelly code. Because Philip's desire to be a playwright is destined to lead to failure, he should never have gone beyond the thinking stage since *any* effort would inevitably be a waste of time. The culprits are Philip's own ignorance of self and the friends and relatives who mindlessly encourage the hopelessly amateur writer to try his luck on the stage. There can be no compromise about problems like this one since trying to do something for which a person is simply not qualified can lead only to cruel disillusionment and waste: "It's sad to waste so many years in a lost cause."[1] One of the two gracious ladies who serve as the play's message-bearers counsels Philip: "There are millions of people all over the world that are spoiling their lives regretting that they didn't *do* something, or *take up* something, or keep on with something; when it's the blessing of God that the majority of them did just what they did."[2]

Kelly said he wrote the play as a response to the "big problem in this country of kids being stage struck. There are thousands of Philips in the land."[3] Like many Kelly characters, therefore, Philip is designed as an object lesson; and the play assumes that ministerial tone that hovers over all of Kelly's work. What gives the play its peculiar slant is not its didactic intent, but the subject the playwright has chosen to be didactic about. Stage-struck people are hardly a national problem, but Kelly treats them as if they were. John Mason Brown noted the discrepancy between the play's light matter and its solemn manner: "*Philip Goes Forth* is a light comedy

of George Kelly's writing which, as he has written it, turns out to be
a very heavy one indeed."[4] Francis Fergusson had the same complaint:

It seems that Mr. Kelly intended to write about a solemn, almost a religious
"going forth," and that the only quest he could think of was that of a young
playwright. . . . In trying to find a contemporary theme, he had to pretend
that playmaking is a business of very serious import, and he had to assume
that it matters to anybody what becomes of young men like Philip. I should
say that Mr. Kelly . . . with an ambition which disdains the thin artificiality
of Broadway comedy, was in the unheroic dilemma of being all dressed up
and no place to go.[5]

If Kelly has made too much of Philip's theatrical ambitions and
failures, he has not done so in a cruel way. "Philip is a *sad*, not a
harsh, portrait," Kelly said;[6] and the play's satire is firm yet gentle.
Some critics, always on the alert for Kelly's famed misogyny,
suggested that, had Philip been Philippa, the censure would have
been less moderate. Written in a muted, mellow tone, the play is a
stern but kindly sermon: Philip is misguided, but he is likable; he is
unaffected; he has none of the foolishness, for instance, of the
women in *The Torch-Bearers*. He is simply blind to himself, and the
business of the play is to open his eyes.

Philip's being a likable character softens, of course, the satire
directed at him as a would-be playwright who does not have the
necessary talent. But the play's mellowness is also achieved through
the characters of Philip's "instructors": in Mrs. Randolph, Philip's
aunt, and in Mrs. Ferris, Philip's landlady in New York, Kelly has
created two wise and serene ladies. In the tradition of Fred Ritter,
the disgruntled husband in *The Torch-Bearers*, these two ladies
perform the traditional choric function of *raisonneurs*: they lecture
and educate Philip and, presumably, the audience. Though their
emphasizing the play's lesson indicates perhaps too much of the
playwright's worry about getting his point across the footlights, they
are the most ingratiating observers in all his work.

In accents strong and clear, the two women alternate in underlining the meaning of Philip's attempt to fulfill his aspirations. For
example, Mrs. Randolph explains to Philip that,"—To come back at
all,—in a thing of this kind, is difficult enough. It isn't like mere
failure in an ordinary business;—the very attempt has something in
it of a—going forth; and to return, defeated,—no matter how sin-

cere the effort has been,—has always in it something of an element of the absurd." When Philip tries to defend himself with the argument, "I think that's very little for a man to ask in his life,—to do the thing he wants to do," Mrs. Randolph, the voice of Kelly prudence and sobriety, counters: "I used to think so, Philip,—but I don't anymore. . . . I mean the danger of—wasted years,—and disillusionment; and the loss of enthusiasm for life, generally. Because, you know, very often, Philip, we only *think* we want to do a thing. . . ."

After Philip has been in New York, and has become more interested in his job as a buyer for an import firm than in his writing, Mrs. Ferris, a retired actress—a woman who had "it" and who knows the signs of the true theater artist ("And believe *me*, Philip, they are *not* on *you*.")—absorbs Mrs. Randolph's role of counselor: "I've been watching you very closely around here for the past six months;—and I've found out something more important than whether you can write or not . . . and that is that you don't *want* to write. . . . You're a businessman, Philip,—gone wrong. Because you listened to some damn fool back home, or at school, or somewhere else—that told you you ought to get in on this thing. . . you realized that it was *work*, like any other job; and work that *you* are not even *interested* in."

To underscore the theme of the artist as person of instinct, Kelly fills Mrs. Ferris' boardinghouse with three exemplary artistic types: Mr. Haines, a competent, but inescapably second-rate pianist who aspires to the top and whose frustrations end in suicide (a Kelly slip, the suicide is pure melodrama that keys a contrived Act II climax); Shronk, "an undersized little fatty," one of those mindless encouragers whom Kelly so dislikes, a hanger-on with a textbook knowledge of playwriting; and La Krail, a poet who, unlike the other boarders, is supposed to represent The Real Thing. However, Kelly errs in her portrayal in that she is too broadly conceived; she seems in fact to be a burlesque of the quivering, supremely sensitive poet who is rapturous about sunsets, purple damasks, and roses. After the audience has been encouraged to laugh at her, it is told by Mrs. Ferris that in La Krail a true greatness resides.[7]

Recognizing the severity of his lecture, Kelly tries to soften the play with a sly twist at the end. Philip's father, who has always been sternly opposed to Philip's "theater nonsense," appears at the boardinghouse in a becalmed mood; and, when Philip agrees to return home, Mr. Eldridge says, "As soon as we get home,—I will deliver into *your* hands,—the first sixteen pages of a play that *I* tried to write one time."[8] Kelly also tries to counter the prevailing austerity with the suggestions of a romance between Philip and a young lady who thinks "there's something of the artist" in Philip. Their scenes together—at the end of Act I, immediately prior to Philip's "going forth," and at the end of the play, immediately before the father-son reconciliation—are charming, light, almost conventionally romantic; they are, at any rate, the closest approximation of romantic scenes that Kelly ever wrote.

Kelly is trying, then, to be as sympathetic and as kind as possible. Despite his efforts, however, the play's thesis alienated and offended many critics. Everyone agreed that "fortunately Mr. Kelly is too sure of his place in our theater to run much risk of being hoist by his own petard. Mr. Kelly, unlike the hero of his play, has what it takes to be a playwright";[9] but, "when Mr. Kelly is preaching about the futility of worshiping the Muse he can be infernally patronizing. It is all a little too smug in its attitude. . . . Mr. Kelly is looking down from a great height."[10] Brooks Atkinson, who was especially irritated by Kelly's message, thought he was being entirely unfair to the theater novice: "To discourage the neophytes about coming to New York and trying their fortune with the arts is to accept considerable responsibility. They bring us hope and faith day by day, and sometimes they bring us ability. . . . Whether they are full-flowered dramatists or muddy-mettled romantics, they bring us fervor and enthusiasm, faith and ambition, and a willingness to learn. What makes this department so disgruntled with Mr. Kelly's new play is the absence of these enchantments in its point of view."[11]

The play's pattern of alternately hitting hard and then softening the sermon is well intentioned, but it nevertheless indicates a division that runs through Kelly's work between the broad and the subtle, the obvious and the ambiguous, the flat and the round— between the undignified comic techniques of vaudeville on the one hand and the higher reaches of Ibsenite drama toward which Kelly aspired on the other. Like virtually all his work, *Philip Goes Forth* is "not pure in its genre";[12] it is "half-satirical, half-serious. . . . The situation is bursting with comic possibilities. But suddenly it all goes flat, the comedy is sprinkled with small but startling tragedy."[13] The common sense of the aunt and the landlady "flattens out the comedy."[14] Moreover, the wavering tone—from comic exaggeration to dead-pan didacticism—is seen particularly in Kelly's fluctuating treatment of Philip's fellow boarders. John Mason Brown pointed out: "Though Mr. Kelly first paints Philip's fellow roomers in terms of the broadest farce—indeed, caricatures them unmercifully—he soon expects us to take them as seriously as he begins to take them himself."[15]

If the solemn moments are not always fully controlled, the play again demonstrates conclusively Kelly's superiority in the lighter register. He may run afoul when he brings in a suicide, or when he has La Krail recite a passage of florid poetry, but he is entirely successful in his comic portrait of Mrs. Oliver, an archetypal Kelly matron. She talks on and on about nothing in particular—bubbles about her imminent European trip, about her own writing proclivities, or about her admiration for Mrs. Ferris' acting. She engages the very sober Mr. Eldridge in light-hearted chit-chat about this and that; she fusses over appointments and the time of day and who said what to whom. Whenever she is on, the play soars.

In addition to Mrs. Oliver, an incidental pleasure of *Philip Goes Forth* is what Kelly reveals through his characters about his own attitudes toward playwriting. Trained in and by the theater rather than in the classroom, Kelly disparages an academic and hence, from his point of view, a cloistered approach to drama when he has Philip relate he had "read a book while . . . up there [at college] by Professor De Lostro, who is one of the authorities of the world on playwriting, in which he says—'why not the happy ending? Since we are undoubtedly called to an ultimate happiness, perhaps the so-called 'Happy Ending,' so anathematized of critics, is nearer to the ultimate drama than that frustration and misery that closes our limited experience.' " Shronk, the theater-textbook expert, is always prepared to recite the jargon that "I don't think Philip always knows just what to do with it [spiritual content]; but I think if he ever finds out, there'll simply be no stopping him; for he's got everything else at his fingertips. Psychology of emotional reaction,—sense of obligatory scene,—his architecture is sound; and he's absolutely uncanny on his symbols."

Kelly mocks the ambitions of fledgling authors: the foolhardy reliance on personal experience in Philip's statement that "I could write about my own *life*, as far as that goes. There'd be enough drama in that to make a half a dozen plays." And Kelly is as unsparing in his criticism of the sophomoric play of intellectual fantasy; for,

no experimenter himself, Kelly had little patience for avant-garde
self-indulgences. When, for example, Shronk and Philip are working on a Chinese fantasy, Shronk counsels Philip: "It isn't as though
you were held to any fixed structure. That's what's the matter with
the drama today,—there's too much technique and not enough
whimsy. . . . Instead of having Ambition find Fame in the Tower
of Life, have him find Death. Do you get it? And there's your Note
of Irony, too, that Professor De Lostro speaks about—Life mocking
at Human Aspiration." Kelly is also opposed to plays that are "just
life," neither beginning nor ending anywhere; and one of Philip's
plays "isn't about anything in particular. . . . It just keeps on
going."

But Kelly does allow Philip one sound observation about the
theater: "Rhythm. It's a musical quality in the writing, you know.
But it's very important; because it's a thing that can't be acquired. I
mean, you either have it or you haven't." And, because Philip
clearly lacks the sense of rhythm—that rhythm which illuminates
Kelly's own work and which never failed him even in plays of mixed
merit like *Philip Goes Forth*[16]—Kelly advises his character to return
home to the world of business where he belongs.

II   Reflected Glory

Though *Reflected Glory* was written in 1929, it was greeted as a
new play when it opened on Broadway in 1936.[17] The opening was
something of an occasion on two counts: *Reflected Glory* was Kelly's
first produced play since *Philip Goes Forth*, and it was the first
major New York role for Tallulah Bankhead following her triumphs
in London. As a double comeback, the production was a society
event: "At the Morosco Theater . . . the season's best bejeweled
audience gathered to extend a warm welcome to both star and
vehicle."[18] Most of the reviewers concentrated their praise on the
actress rather than on the play, and there is a kind of justice in doing
so since *Reflected Glory* is Kelly's least personal play and since it
represents his writing more nearly to formula than in any other
work of his.

When Kelly left New York in 1931, he was angry because his last
several plays had not taken, and he announced to the press that the
New York stage has "practically no appeal right now for the writer
interested in a serious, analytical study of characters and situations."[19] Because of this assertion, it is surprising that Kelly chose

Reflected Glory as his comeback play, for it is neither a demanding nor a fully serious consideration of its characters or its theme. Kelly had certainly written star parts before—Harriet Craig and Aubrey Piper are that, but all of the parts in those two plays are rich in "points" and "business" and only a careless director would permit the plays to become star turns. *Reflected Glory*, however, does not provide Muriel Flood, its actress-heroine, with any truly colorful or weighty opponents—a unique situation in a Kelly play; and the result is that Muriel has the stage to herself. Tallulah, of course, took full advantage of this opportunity; and Kelly was overshadowed by his star for the first and only time in his career. Although not actually the case, it certainly looked as if Kelly had written "the typical Bankhead play. . . . It is," noted Wolcott Gibbs, "the sort of play in which the other characters just sit around, talking in expectant undertones, until it amuses the star to come in and shout at them in her justly celebrated voice."[20] As written, the part of Muriel Flood has some subtlety, some minor modulations on the stock temperamental actress role; but the writing is not distinctive enough to counter the attack of a temperamental actress like Tallulah Bankhead. As a result, the play became the familiar "exhibit" of a high-strung actress playing a high-strung actress, "stalking about on her heels, slapping the furniture to accentuate her outbursts, lowering her voice to a sepulchral baritone, leaning backward at an angle of 30° while combing her hair."[21]

Reflected Glory shows the Kelly touch around the edges, but the basic formulation of its argument is disappointingly commonplace. "The action is, moreover, as stereotyped as the central character," complained Joseph Wood Krutch. "There remain of course two possible explanations. The one is that the original play was revised out of existence to suit Miss Bankhead, who probably does not want to be anything less than a heroine. The other is that even Mr. Kelly, despite the fact that he managed to emerge originally out of vaudeville, has got submerged in Hollywood. In any case he has obviously lost somewhere the uncommon touch."[22]

Reflected Glory centers, then, about an actress who is torn between a career and romance, for, dedicated to her profession, she nonetheless has all the womanly desires for marriage and a family. In an altogether workmanlike way, Kelly provides her with three men to choose among. Tom Howard, the young man from back home, is "one of those people that a play is a show to him, and that's all";[23] he is provincial, well-meaning, but hopelessly outside the center of things for either Kelly or his character. When Muriel admits that she may not be "temperamentally suited" to marriage, Tom classifies all women together; unable to make exceptions for unusual talent, he maintains that "there never was a woman in the world that wasn't temperamentally suited to marriage," though "there might be certain types of men."

Leonard Wall has quite the opposite character of Tom Howard. A stage-door Johnny, he likes Muriel *because* she is an actress. "I've admired all kinds of women," he says. "But there's always been an enormous attraction for me about a woman that has what I call— *color*. It's kind of an irresistible thing; I never tire of watching her." Unfortunately, something of Wall's vulgar worship of glamor creeps into Kelly's own homage to Muriel.

The third contender for Muriel's affections is her producer. Hanlon, a gruff sort, is in love with the theater ("it can bring a little inspiration and beauty" to "a lot of people"); and he recognizes in Muriel what Mrs. Ferris (in *Philip Goes Forth*) claims for La Krail—the inspiration and the instincts of the born artist. Hanlon, like Kelly, has "the most uncanny sense of when it's [acting] right. And a perfect *worship* of anybody that's able to do it right."[24]

Too attracted to the stage to live the suburban life with Tom and disillusioned by Wall's use of her to get into glamorous circles, Muriel is left at the end without a man, except for her wrangling relationship with Hanlon. In the play's final moments, Muriel and Hanlon are absorbed in working out a detail about a stage movement—and their preoccupation with stage business saves them. Their involvement recalls the memorable descent into trivia at the end of Kelly's early one-act, *One of Those Things;* for the results in both are the same—the easing of pressure by not looking deeply into personal problems, and, therefore, the loss of anxiety by attention to trivial matters.

The unromantic ending—the choice of vocation over marriage— gives the play its Kelly flavoring. If too many of the basic conflicts seem merely to conform to conventional patterns, the underlying theme of vocation and the ascetic dedication to work represent Kelly's personalization of the material. Muriel is an artist; and that means, according to Kelly, that she is an exceptional person who must bear exceptional burdens. Kelly responded to the critics who had accused him of writing a formula play by saying that "he realizes that while the subject has been used in many variants before, he thinks he has given it a slant, showing the tragedy of a life that has been overshadowed by a talent."[25] Miss Flood's maid, Hattie, speaks the Kelly theme: "Well, I guess certain people are cut out to do certain things, Miss Flood, and they've just got to do them. And if the things are important enough, I guess they're more important than *they* are." *Reflected Glory* is thus written on the Shavian theme of the special obligations and denials demanded of the talented person. Like Shaw's Marchbanks, Muriel Flood is a true artist for whom marriage and its conventional securities are positive hindrances.

Hattie and Stella Sloane, Muriel's chum and her perennial supporting player, are the spokeswomen for the playwright's common sense. They comprise the play's unromantic Kelly chorus:

Miss Sloane: Don't delude yourself with the idea that love is enough,—for a whole life, I mean; because it isn't.—It's like everything else in the world,—it's born, and it lives, and it dies. And then, what are you going to do?

Hattie: I wish to God I'd never had any life *outside* the theater. . . . I've at least had peace and my own dollar since I've been in it; and that's something I never had before. This talk about gettin' married and havin' some man to take care of you is a laugh to *me*. They'll take care of your money,— that's about the only thing they'll take care of. . . . *I* want to tell *you* there's nothin' in God's world like bein' able to go home to your own room at night and know that there's goin' to be nobody there to meet you.

Through Hattie and Stella, Kelly is vindicating the independent woman. Although the play reflects his usual anti-marriage bias, the terms are reversed: it is now the men who are the obstacles to self-fulfillment rather than the women. Indeed, *Reflected Glory* is a Kelly play with three admirable women: Hattie and Stella, who are entirely self-sufficient, know how to make their own way; and Kelly respects them for it. Muriel wavers, but she learns during the course of the play that she too must become self-sufficient. These women without men give the play its curiously sexless atmosphere; it is as if the theater is a nunnery that channels all passion into its exalted purposes.

This religious dedication to the theater—the placement of theater above personal considerations, and the artist's public service considered more important than his private satisfactions—indicates

Kelly's love of his profession. *Reflected Glory* is his encouragement to the true artist, just as *Philip Goes Forth* was written to discourage the big-city amateur and *The Torch-Bearers* and *The Flattering Word* were written to satirize something even worse—the provincial amateur. That Kelly has not made anyone believe in the special greatness of Muriel—she seems merely a conventional theatrical type, the sort of *grande dame prima donna* who cannot play "an emotional scene in a dress without a train," and whose rhythm is affected because her maid let her go on stage opening night without her bracelets—is the play's central failure. Kelly does not go deeply enough into the nature of the actress; he neglects thorough consideration of the qualities necessary for great acting. There are scattered approaches to the subject, but Kelly keeps his distance, as if such discussion would be too intellectual within the context of a popular drama.

Philip Goes Forth indicates much more about Kelly's attitude toward theater than any of his other plays; it is a more theoretical play than *Reflected Glory* which, since it is an homage to the art of the theater and to the people who make the theater an art, ought properly to include more observations on the nature of acting and on theatrical style. Stark Young's complaint about the intellectual thinness of *Reflected Glory* is, alas, appropriate: "The play . . . reminds us again how much a son of the theater he is—the theater taken as a craft, a practical manner of entertaining audiences, a popular medium that either does not intend to do much thinking or could not if it tried."[26]

Conceivably, if certain of Hattie's and Hanlon's speeches in praise of Muriel Flood were removed, the play could be turned into a satire of the temperamental actress rather than a vindication of her. At the end of Act I, the leading characters in both *Reflected Glory* and *Philip Goes Forth* arrange themselves in extravagant, self-conscious theatrical poses:

[Philip] moves forward to the chair at the right and rests his hands upon the back of it. The smile fades from his face, his expression becomes set, and his eyes climb to a point far up and away off. His chest lifts slowly, and he gazes, starry-eyed,—the young crusader.

Flood raises her eyes and looks away off,—almost unconsciously assuming an attitude appropriate to the dignity of her future greatness.

Since Philip's pose is unearned, his sense of self-importance is being satirized; but Muriel, presumably, is The Real Thing. Yet the similarity of her gesture to Philip's suggests the closeness to satire of Kelly's concept of the great actress. Some of the critics, in fact, declined to accept Muriel for what she was intended to represent, preferring instead to regard her character, as well as the play, as "half-burlesque," as "gentle vaudeville."[27]

But in its theme of vocation and in its skirting of a conventionally romantic happy ending, *Reflected Glory* contains Kelly's personal variations on a formula. And the tone, too—"careful, semi-chucklesome, semi-melancholy"[28]—is distinctively his. If we compare this subdued, even rather dainty, portrait of back-stage life with Kaufman and Ferber's *The Royal Family* or with Kaufman and Hart's *Stage Door*, we can see that Kelly's play avoids the flamboyance, the hectic activity, the gags, and the wisecracks of those two commercial plays about theater types. Kelly's characters are much more circumspect and formal, and their preoccupation with domestic detail and trivia is especially delightful. Hattie's opening movements in each act are the most enjoyable sections of the play as she fusses about props, buttons, and letters. In fact, Hattie, dry, efficient, bustling, loquacious, and snoopy, is Kelly's most fully realized servant. She takes up more of the play's time than almost any other playwright would allow; but—in her small, endless preoccupations; her clinging to the surface; her disciplined routine; her "line of talk"—the Kelly rhythm comes through strong and clear.

CHAPTER 7

The Kelly Matron

A FTER *Reflected Glory*, Kelly again retired to California. In 1938, he directed a West Coast revival of *The Torch-Bearers*; but he wrote no plays until the mid-1940's when he engaged in a flurry of theatrical activity: *The Deep Mrs. Sykes* in 1945, *The Fatal Weakness* in 1946, and the direction of *Craig's Wife* in 1947 which closed his career in the theater. There were rumors of new productions in the late 1940's and early 1950's: Ina Claire was to star in his high comedy, *When All Else Fails;* and there was some talk of the production of a tragedy, *Can Two Walk Together?* But Kelly could cast neither play satisfactorily: "They're real theater," he said; but "they couldn't be cast in today's theater; you don't have the pick that you did in the 1920's."[1]

Between the 1938 revival of *The Torch-Bearers* and the 1945 production of *The Deep Mrs. Sykes*, Kelly worked on some film scripts in an advisory capacity but on nothing he wished to be associated with his name; he traveled extensively; and he thought about ideas for plays. Kelly's prolonged absence from the theater gave him a near-legendary stature,[2] but admiring critics scolded him for the infrequency of his contributions. "No human faculty can remain robust without exercise," warned John Chapman. "It is like a cultured, clear-thinking person who has deliberately starved himself for a long period—awfully nice and all that, but wobbly on the pins and blue around the gills. A good big mess of meat and potatoes would help."[3]

When Kelly finally returned to playwriting, the two plays he delivered—*The Deep Mrs. Sykes* and *The Fatal Weakness*—were very close in spirit and theme. *The Deep Mrs. Sykes*, the more astringent of the two works, is drawing-room comedy mixed with sober moral conclusions and hints of personal tragedy; *The Fatal Weakness*, pure high comedy, is Kelly's most polished and glittering contribution to the genre. But both plays, set in an unmistakably upper-middle-class milieu, are fundamentally character studies in the manner of *Craig's Wife*. Neither is as unpleasant as Kelly's Pulitzer Prize play, but both have as their aim the exposure of some feminine folly—a quirk of the feminine psyche as only Kelly can conceive it.

In *The Deep Mrs. Sykes*, Kelly attacks woman's intuition, a subject he had already touched upon in his early one-act, *The Weak Spot*, and, glancingly, in the characterization of Mrs. J. Duro Pampinelli in *The Torch-Bearers*. Kelly said that "Mrs. Sykes is a tough character, she's a woman egotist, a much more dangerous person than the male egotist because she always hides behind her intuition."[4] In *The Fatal Weakness*, Kelly's censure of a female foible is less acid; his Mrs. Espenshade, who attends every wedding that she possibly can, and who enjoys a good cry at all of them, is an incurably and foolishly romantic matron. Unlike Mrs. Sykes, Mrs. Espenshade is merely silly rather than dangerous; but, because Kelly implies that both women are victims of their peculiarly feminine maladjustments, they are therefore conceived in the Kelly "humors" fashion. They represent particular types, and the definition and criticism of them are at the center of the plays.

The two plays are written in Kelly's final manner which, like Henry James', is a flourishing of the eccentricities of his peculiar genius. The plays deal, therefore, with types that are significantly less universal than the show-off and the overly meticulous housekeeper; and their off-center characters are presented in a less conventional dramatic framework than Kelly's popular plays of the 1920's. Indeed, *The Deep Mrs. Sykes* and *The Fatal Weakness* are surely two of the oddest plays ever to receive Broadway production. Those unfamiliar with Kelly—those who come to the plays fresh and uninstructed—are likely to regard the proceedings as something in the nature of a code for which the explanatory key is missing. Set in drawing rooms, the plays have the surface look of conventional upper-class drama; and they are exactly what people who hate the theater hate—polite conversation and fancily dressed people standing around with cocktail glasses and cigarette holders. Impatient strangers to Kelly's work are likely to be puzzled, perhaps infuriated, by the fact that nothing very definite and certainly nothing conventionally dramatic transpires among these chatty, smartly dressed people.

Both plays—but *Mrs. Sykes* in particular—are made up of meandering and repetitious exposition, catty insinuations, oblique confrontations. Marching sublimely to the beat of his own music, Kelly sidesteps audience expectation; the plays avoid firm resolutions just as they bypass obligatory scenes. Louis Kronenberger nicely summarized Kelly's idiosyncratic temperament; to him, Kelly refuses "to be bullied by theater conventions, [he insists] on doing exactly what he wants—whether it be letting a souse repeat herself at considerable length, or having people stand around while somebody plays the piano off-stage. . . . [His is] the integrity of a man who knows what effects *he* wants, and doesn't give a hoot about the effects audiences are supposed to respond to. That is a rare habit among playwrights."[5]

I The Deep Mrs. Sykes

The Deep Mrs. Sykes is structured with such a violation of the principles of the well-made play that its form could almost be considered experimental; and Kelly develops his materials with the utmost leisure. Like Mrs. Craig before her, Mrs. Sykes has just returned from an out-of-town visit; and, possessed of the disinterested curiosity that is the habitual preoccupation of the Kelly matron, she questions her servants and her husband about events that have transpired in her absence. Significantly, the play opens with a question: "Who is that man out there with Mr. Sykes, Ada?"[6] The principal development during Mrs. Sykes' absence, it turns out, has been a dinner party at the Club given by their neighbor, Mr. Taylor, for the new Mrs. Taylor, who is, in addition to being lovely and charming, an accomplished pianist.

At the dinner, Mrs. Taylor had casually mentioned that her favorite flowers are white lilacs; and when she subsequently receives an anonymously sent bouquet of white lilacs, she assumes they were sent by Dr. and Mrs. Fentriss. Graciously, but unwisely, Mrs. Taylor sends them a note of appreciation, only to be told that the Fentrisses did not send the flowers. Being an hysterical woman, and the town drunk as well, Mrs. Fentriss suspects that her husband *did* after all send the flowers; and, when the intuition-proud Mrs. Sykes intimates that *she* knows the identity of the sender, Mrs. Fentriss simply must know who he is.

The sender of the white lilacs has now been elevated to the role of Mrs. Taylor's lover. The instigator of the rumor, Mrs. Sykes herself, denying later the authorship of the scandalous suggestion, claims that she identified the sender merely as Mrs. Taylor's "protégé." While Mrs. Fentriss is busy convincing herself that Dr. Fentriss sent the flowers, Mrs. Sykes is certain that *Mr.* Sykes is the scoundrel. Both ladies, of course, are wrong; for Mrs. Sykes' son Ralph, enamored of the charming Mrs. Taylor, had sent the lilacs. When Mrs. Sykes is confronted with this knowledge, she refuses to believe it; she claims that good, kind-hearted Ralph is merely shielding his father. Both Mr. Sykes and Ralph's wife Ethel, who is the real "deep Mrs. Sykes," know about Ralph's fascination and both try to convince him to preserve his marriage. But Mrs. Sykes remains to the end convinced of the accuracy of her intuition.

Told straightforwardly, this play seems a minor comedy of manners, a satire of gossipy clubwomen that is rather fully and even conventionally plotted. But, as Kelly kneads and nurtures his material, it assumes a quite distinctive coloring. First of all, the plot as such is merely sandwiched between, and on the periphery of, Kelly small talk at its most extravagantly leisurely elaboration. For example, a maid comes in bringing Mrs. Sykes' spectacles; a butler brings in the usual glass of water; Sykes tells an unresponsive Mrs. Sykes a story about a politician who wanted to change the world and whose voice couldn't even reach the front row; and Mrs. Sykes comments, *en passant* (practically all the dialogue is *en passant*, for that matter), about Mr. Sykes' reading material: "Can't you find anything more adult to read, Ozzie, than continental humor?" And she recommends some edifying reading:

Mrs. Sykes: You never even opened *Staring into Space* and I paid eight dollars for it. . . . It's an enormously instructive work; and there are certain things in it that I think you should absolutely know about. . . . there's a chapter there on shooting stars, for one thing,—that is one of the most breathtaking documents I've ever read in my life. It made me feel as though I were actually there.
Mr. Sykes: Actually where?
Mrs. Sykes: Why, wherever they're *shooting* I suppose.

When Myrtle, Cyril, Lorrie Fentriss, and Ralph stop by after a wedding, they talk sardonically about the much-married bride and about the prospective honeymoon:

Mrs. Sykes: They're going to Phoenix, Arizona, aren't they?
Myrtle: So he said.
Cyril: He told *me* they were going to the West Indies, Myrtle.

Myrtle: Well, *he* thinks Arizona's in the West Indies, darling, don't be silly.
Mrs. Sykes: Is it true that he's an Eskimo?
Myrtle: No, dear, he's an aviator. Well, I mean he's not an Eskimo, anyway.

Mrs. Sykes, à propos of nothing in particular, talks about her trip.

Mrs. Sykes: I've been out in Milwaukee visiting my family.
Cyril: Milwaukee, Wisconsin, you mean?
Mrs. Sykes: Yes, I have a Mother and two brothers out there.

When Mr. Sykes mentions his failed ambition of being a singer, Mrs. Sykes (with shades of Mrs. Craig) responds sharply: "But you'd have had to go away some place . . . I mean, to Paris, or Rome, or one of those places—where they *allow* it. Well, I mean it would never be tolerated in a quiet neighborhood like this,—you know that as well as I do." Mrs. Sykes mentions that *she* wanted to be a balloonist ("I think it was the detachment of the thing that appealed to me"). This talk of vocations, failed and otherwise, prompts mention of Mrs. Taylor's "line":

Mrs. Sykes: She's an actress of some kind, isn't she?
Mrs. Fentriss: No, she's a musician.
Myrtle: A pianist, dear.
Mrs. Fentriss: She plays the piano.

The "intrigue" of the white lilacs is not introduced until half-way into the act.

Act I concludes with its closest approximation of conventional drama—Mrs. Sykes confides to Ralph about his father and requests Ralph to keep a close watch on him for the sake of the family. Mrs. Sykes takes a cold-blooded attitude toward the entire matter: "This is a realistic world. So I don't want you to be too hard on [your father]: for most every man is victimized at one time or another in his life by some foolish vanity." And after her revelation, Kelly, working always against melodrama and the large gesture, has her turn nonchalantly to trivia: "And before I forget it, Ralph,—I have a box of that candy here from Milwaukee."

In Act II, another gathering of the group occurs in another meticulous, elegantly appointed drawing room. The action is similarly pockmarked by the Kelly business, but the most idiosyncratic incident is the moment when Mrs. Fentriss, hot and flushed, swirls from the dining room into the living room, ready to do battle with the maddeningly secretive Mrs. Sykes—and what does she say? "I like steps this way,—down into a drawing room. I wish that room of mine had them." In his characteristically precise stage directions, Kelly notes that "the floor of the drawing room proper is twelve inches below the level of the wide hallway which runs along at the back."

Just as a confrontation between Mrs. Fentriss and Mrs. Sykes seems about to begin, the men enter (from the library, of course); and the talk turns to social niceties—to the pleasures of music and the graceful beauty of Mrs. Sykes' three harps. The drawing room is cleared; the guests are to hear an impromptu Sibelius recital by Mr. Manzoni; but Mr. Sykes remains behind in order to chastise Mrs. Sykes for her "assumptions of supernatural powers to support any statement that she [makes]." But *this* confrontation is interrupted by returning guests, and the subject turns to the sad news about the Taylors' moving to New York. In a blind rage, Mrs. Fentriss rushes into the snow in order to confront her husband with her certain conviction of his infidelity; she falls, breaks an arm, and is rushed to the hospital; Mrs. Sykes and Myrtle decide that their place is with her, personal differences notwithstanding; and their departure is accompanied by the most elaborate set of good-byes in the Kelly canon.

After Mrs. Sykes' chatty departure, the play again concentrates on the main intrigue with the closing interview between the legitimately deep and wise Mrs. Sykes, who has seen all, and Ralph, who needs to be told all. As in the endings of *The Show-Off* and *Philip Goes Forth*, Kelly makes light of his serious theme with flippant irony. Ralph gushes: "You know, it wouldn't surprise *me*, Ethel, if *you* were intuitive, too! . . . I mean, you knew about me! And you knew about *Dad* knowing about me. . . . I don't know how you could have known about all those things unless you're—"

Quite understandably, the critics, who didn't know what to make of this curious play, complained that "not in a long while has a stage been so filled with unpleasant people";[7] the play has "a sharp edge but no point; a powerful meaningless play";[8] "we may have seen worse plays but never one as enraging. . . . You can take your pick of the points the whole thing tries to prove: don't come from Milwaukee, don't live in a small town, don't get married, don't get your feet wet."[9]

Kappo Phelan's complaint catches much of the play's spirit:

For my part, I do not think any play possible which is built entirely of exposition. . . . As there are some fourteen different characters, it follows that whatever infinitesimal circumstance transpires on the stage must be learned fourteen different times by the house. Fourteen different times we were made acquainted with the botanical intrigue, fourteen different times with the certain knowledge that so-and-so drinks, fourteen different times that Mr. Taylor was taking Mrs. Taylor to live in New York, and (the nadir) fourteen different times with the fact that Sibelius was about to be, was being, and had been played, in the den.[10]

The play does lack thematic focus, for Kelly is continually diverted from his character study of Mrs. Sykes by the polite and meandering (and delightfully illogical) small talk of his stageful of chatterboxes. And, at the end, after having attacked feminine intuition, Kelly introduces a curious plea for the status quo that contradicts what has preceded it. Mr. Sykes cautions Ralph: "You have a wife and child;—and a very nice position in this town for a young fellow of your age." He cites his own perseverance as an example to follow:

I met the only woman that I have ever really loved—at the party the night my engagement to your Mother was announced. . . . And I'm still here. . . . I'm not sorry. For it's taught me a couple of very useful things. And *you* may find them useful, too, as you go along. And one of them is,—that a man isn't so badly off at all when he's married to a woman that's in love with him. . . . And the other thing is,—that there's nothing quite so valuable in a life as a little romance in the offing—one of those things that never dies,—because it's never *quite* allowed to live. . . .

With its concern for appearance, its subservience to the demands of respectability, and its support of the half-lived life, this stodgy morality is more appropriate to the world of Sir Arthur Wing Pinero or Henry Arthur Jones than to the brittle world of the Kelly drawing room. Joseph Wood Krutch, who objected to Mr. Sykes' sermon, considered it "a very weak case for the sacredness of a union irksome to one of the parties, and it is difficult to see who has profited from the preservation of the marriage between the speaker and his despicable mate."[11] Moreover, Kelly has made such a strong case *against* Mrs. Sykes that it is hard indeed to accept Mr. Sykes' conciliatory attitude. As Rosamund Gilder, who voiced the popular objection to the miscalculated prudence of Kelly's denouement, observed: "It is difficult to have any sympathy for a husband who would put up with such arrogance and stupidity, such intolerable rudeness and deep-rooted unkindliness."[12]

Kelly also changes course in his depiction of Mrs. Fentriss. She is perhaps too strongly drawn, too passionate for the rarefied atmosphere of the play. There is indeed something finally tragic about her breakdown in Act II: " . . . the losingest game a woman ever played . . . allowing your husband to live his life at your expense:—and don't you ever do it, Ethel. For he'll *let* you,—if you're fool enough,—don't make any mistake about that." For a moment this anti-woman play becomes anti-male, a fitting, though not entirely integrated, ambiguity for this strange, unclassifiable play of mixed means, half-notes, and tinted tones.

II   The Fatal Weakness

Though Kelly did not intend *The Fatal Weakness* to be his last play (and indeed he has since written four plays, though they remain, unfortunately, both unproduced and unpublished), this work is nonetheless a lovely and gracious swan song. Writing again on the subject of a female eccentricity—the Romantic Type—Kelly is gentle with his heroine. He is really fond of his Mrs. Espenshade, and he subjects her to none of the barbs that he directed at his Mrs. Craigs and Mrs. Sykeses. Mrs. Espenshade is rather fond and rather foolish, but Kelly clearly likes her and he encourages the same response in his audience. Near the end of the play, Mrs. Espenshade remarks that "the art of living is the art of withdrawing gracefully," and Kelly feels that the play lends support to the wisdom and the truth of this statement.[13] Hardly an emphatic or direct demonstration of this point, the play nonetheless has a muted, mellow quality, an essential sanity and serenity, which make it a particularly appropriate final statement.

The idea for *The Fatal Weakness* "came to Mr. Kelly last year while he was reading proof on *The Deep Mrs. Sykes*,"[14] and the closeness of the two plays is readily apparent. They are a complementary pair, but the one has dark tints, and the other has rosy highlights. Both are, in a sense, plays of mystery and intrigue: the question to be solved in *Mrs. Sykes* is the source of the white lilacs sent to Mrs. Taylor; and the question of *The Fatal Weakness* is whether or not Mr. Espenshade is having an affair with a woman osteopath. Since Kelly makes it clear early in the play that he is having one, the tension of *The Fatal Weakness* is considerably less than that of the preceding play in which the identity of the sender of those white lilacs is a trickier puzzle and in which the solution is withheld until farther along in the play.

Like the characters in *The Deep Mrs. Sykes*, the characters of this play satisfy their curiosity by asking each other questions. The asking of questions in both plays is a kind of ritualized ceremony—a very domesticated, very unexotic ceremony, to be sure, but something of a tribal ritual nonetheless. As Mary McCarthy has noted, "In these last plays, the American family is seen as a nomadic integer, inquiring, placing, dating, its only impulse a locative one."[15]

In Mrs. Espenshade's quest to determine her husband's guilt or innocence, she has the expert assistance of Mabel Wentz, one of Kelly's most likable matrons. Fussy, absorbed by trivia, snoopy, and endlessly chatty, she lacks the venom of some of Kelly's other idle women. Though we never see her, Minnie Nichols also helps in the hunt; since Minnie doesn't have anything else to do, or at least nothing she would rather do, she follows Espenshade and his lady doctor for hours and hours.

Though the play's subject of marital infidelity is certainly familiar, Kelly's variations on it are characteristically unconventional and unsentimental. Joseph Wood Krutch, one of the few critics who has proved unfailingly perceptive in judging Kelly's work, noted that "neither the action nor the author's commentary ever falls into any of the familiar grooves one is perpetually expecting it to find. Mr. Kelly rejects all the ready-made patterns which would immediately render his play comfortably classifiable and thus defeats all the easy expectations."[16] Kelly's decidedly original working out of his characters' histories makes it possible for the play to be more than a ladies' matinee item. Discovering her husband's duplicity, Mrs. Espenshade does not try to win him back. Instead, she gives him his freedom without any temperamental scenes or bitter recriminations—without, in fact, any of the standard emotional reactions usually evoked by situations such as this one. She not only lets him go to his lady doctor, she even attends their wedding; for attending weddings—no matter whose—is her particular hobby.[17]

Mrs. Espenshade's wedding fever is lightly ridiculed throughout the play, for Kelly gently mocks her sentimentality. Each curtain (and there are five of them) finds Mrs. Espenshade in some romantic pose or giving voice to a silly romantic notion. At the end of Scene 1, for instance, she tells her maid Anna that she has to see a particular wedding because "their pictures were in last Sunday's paper; and *she* is the most *beautiful* young thing you've ever seen in your life."[18] In Scene 2, her "fatal weakness" is getting involved in the romance of her husband and Dr. Hilton: "They're simply *madly* in love with each other. I've never heard anything so romantic in my life; she was even brought up in an orphanage." At the end of Scene 3, in which she listens to her husband's description of the mountain retreat of his "male" friend, she begins to participate in his revery, pressing a bouquet of roses to her bosom and staring off in wonderment. At the end of Scene 4, she stands, dazed, as Espenshade tells her that she should have been "allowed to just pass through her life as a kind of symbol of the romance that every man'd like to be worthy of"; and he recites a poem that suggests she is the very embodiment of romance. In the finale, as she is about to leave with Mabel Wentz to go to her husband's wedding, she recites the very same poem as she stares off mistily into the middle distance.

But Mrs. Espenshade is self-deluded: she is *not* a romantic lady, but a woman of good common sense, despite her foolish notions, who is always ready with good sound advice. Faced with the imminent collaspse of her marriage, she is admirably calm; since her marriage has failed, she reasons, why not uncomplicate matters by simply letting her husband go? Like her creator, Mrs. Espenshade is an observer rather than a participant; she is so poised and contained because she is so removed—she even takes notes as her son-in-law tells her what he knows about Espenshade's affair. Mrs. Espenshade is, of course, unhappy about losing her husband; but, as Krutch observes, it is her particular quality that "the weight of none of her emotions will ever be more than she can easily bear."[19]

Aside from the irony of Mrs. Espenshade's view of herself in contrast to what she is, the play's ironic tone is enriched by the relationship of Mrs. Espenshade to her daughter. Penny, a woman's liberationist, spouts all the modern theories. She quarrels with her "sentimental" husband: "I think the thing that *annoys* him is that *I* refuse to take marriage seriously—I mean, as a permanent relationship in my life. I think it's an interesting experience." Mrs. Espenshade's response to her "advanced" daughter renders her a close cousin to Kelly's other hard-headed, practical advice-givers:

Mrs. Espenshade: But don't you think you should at least consider which is the more important in your life—the success of your marriage or simply the championship of these opinions of yours?
Penny: I think my personal integrity is more important than either.
Mrs. Espenshade: Oh, stop your silly talk, Penny, I can't listen to any more of it! . . . Are you interested in some other man? Because you talk very much like a woman that might be.
Penny: Can't you conceive of a woman having any other motive in life for *anyting*?
Mrs. Espenshade: Not women that are always talking about their personal integrity I can't.

When confronted with the possibility of her parents' divorce, Penny, not her mother, proves to be the sentimental one: "Well, Mother, you don't mean that you would think of *divorcing* Papa, do you?" Mrs. Espenshade has been educated only too well by her freedom-mongering daughter; and the mother is, ironically, more attuned to her daughter's advanced ideas than the daughter herself. Therefore, while Mrs. Espenshade edges herself gracefully out of her own marriage, she becomes responsible for effecting a reconciliation between Penny and her husband Vernon.

Mrs. Espenshade, a singular woman, is decidedly not one of the universal types of Kelly's earlier plays; and the critics were again puzzled. Everyone praised the charm and comic lightness of Ina Claire's performance as Mrs. Espenshade, but most of the critics couldn't find a foothold in the play itself. As Krutch reflected, "Is this a subject too slight or too elusive for a play? Many would say so. It is, they would argue, rather a subject for a novel or a novelette, for a kind of tenuous analysis somewhat in the manner of Henry James, or at least one of his less weighty followers."[20] To Kappo Phelan,

These women seem to exist in a vacuum . . . as no time nor place-signature marks his program, one is left constantly inwardly inquiring, where IS this weird . . . overdecorated apartment? where ARE these tiny events? Perhaps the nearest I can relate Mr. Kelly's observations to my own will be far-off overheard conferences of Aunts and Grandmothers when discussions of shore vs. mountains for vacations were serious; when servants were steady; and when although innumerable people were dead or dying, no one had ever been killed. I guess it is safest for me to nominate the piece an exercise in nostalgia.[21]

Critics were bothered by the lack of action—"its fatal weakness will be in a script that contains more words than a dictionary and less action than a Stepin Fetchit saunter"[22]—and by the slender theme, a criticism expressed in this way by one critic: "Mr. Kelly's new piece is . . . considerably lighter than air."[23] For some, the play indicated that Kelly belonged to a past generation; he was out of step with the times.

For all its tiny events, its minor ambiguities and reversals, and its contextless setting, *The Fatal Weakness* is a delight for those attuned to the Kelly pace and tone. This play is the most urbane and gracious achievement of a singular playwright.

III *Conclusion*

On the occasion of the popular 1967 revival of *The Show-Off*, Jack Kroll, writing in *Newsweek*, commented: "George Kelly . . . is . . . a genuine sensibility, functioning strongly and in good faith within its limits, and not shooting for the cheesy moon."[24] Though Kelly always confined his plays to a few repeated themes, character types, and settings; though he never tried to write experimental or deep plays; though, in short, his temperament was directly opposite to Eugene O'Neill's, Kelly is not finally a minor artist or simply a popular entertainer. Hardly a dramatist of ideas, Kelly always wrote his plays to *enforce* ideas, usually moral concepts that are noticeable for their modesty and homeliness.

Though he is known primarily as the author of a favorite American comedy (*The Show-Off*), Kelly did not like to think of himself as a "comedian," and he altogether rejected the designation of a writer of farce. His greatest success was with satire, but Kelly also wrote melodrama, tragedy, high comedy, and plays of the middle range that the French call *drames*. Though he began his career in vaudeville, writing for general American audiences, and launched his Broadway career with three commercial plays in a row, he aspired toward higher levels and refused to capitalize on his clearly established ability to entertain.

Impatient with popular acclaim, yet neither deep nor probing enough to qualify as an intellectual writer, Kelly occupies a distinctly middle range. Serious critics like Stark Young, Joseph Wood Krutch, Mary McCarthy, and Louis Kronenberger appreciated Kelly; but they treated him as an oddity and a curiosity, as something of an American Primitive, rather than as a full-fledged man of letters.

Though critics sometimes compared his plays to those of Ibsen, Strindberg, and Chekhov, the dramatists closest to him in tone and thematic concerns are probably Philip Barry, S. N. Behrman, and Sidney Howard; but the similarities are never more than superficial. It is difficult to place Kelly in any tradition. He began in vaudeville, and he is certainly indebted to his early training for his sense of timing and for his overall theatrical acumen. He is part of that colorful theatrical decade of the 1920's in which, led by O'Neill, American drama took giant steps forward. Kelly's period of greatest acclaim and activity spanned the 1920's, but his plays are not thematically rooted in any particular period; he is not a writer of the 1920's the way, for instance, Clifford Odets can be said to be a writer of the 1930's.

Kelly's plays only indirectly reflect the spirit of their times. His comedies of the 1920's, in fact, in which his characters are concerned with financial security, seem more connected to the Depression than to the Jazz Age. Primarily character studies, the plays have a private as opposed to social focus. Kelly is concerned with enduring American types; and his materialistic, security-conscious characters do not necessarily reflect a particular era in American history. The types of the show-off and the immaculate housekeeper are with us still, and Kelly's examinations of trouble-making matrons and put-upon husbands are no more dated or isolated now than they were when they were first presented to theatergoers.

Kelly's work suggests his impatience with certain basic human follies, and the social content of his plays can be reduced to some plain and Puritanical precepts: the valuable citizen is the one who works with competence at his job (Kelly thinks the theater is the highest profession, but he respects anyone who does well the job for which he is suited); who keeps order within his home (and doing so usually means keeping the wife within her place); and who respects the demands of the community. Kelly's ethic is conservative and basic; he respects order, common sense, the essential decencies. The Kelly hero is the undominated, unromantic character who mocks departures from practicality, integrity, and professionalism.

Kelly's idiosyncratic writing requires from the reader a certain amount of patience and flexibility. Because his plays are so specialized and eccentric, they have perhaps more of a coterie than a universal appeal. But for those who are willing to comprehend Kelly, the plays offer generous rewards. Kelly, in fact, merits much more attention than he has received. His dialogue, his theater business, and his controlled rhythm are unfailingly graceful. Kelly is a miniature portraitist of American manners; and, within its own self-imposed limits, his vision is shrewd and rigorous. He is a moralist who mixes his homely sermons with droll, ironic laughter, and his manners plays with their didactic underpinnings are among the most distinctively stylized works in the American repertory. Kelly's position in American drama is unique and it is high.

Notes and References

Preface

1. Mary McCarthy, "George Kelly," *Mary McCarthy's Theater Chronicles 1937–1962* (New York, 1963), p. 97.

Chapter One

1. Personal interview with George Kelly, January 24, 1971, Sun City, California (hereafter referred to as personal interview).
2. Anon. *Time*, "George Kelly Returns to Broadway," XLVI (April 2, 1945): 61.
3. Florence Crowder, "Up From Vaudeville to the Front Rank of American Dramatists," *Letters*, V (February, 1932): 29.
4. Personal interview.
5. *Ibid*.
6. Bill Corum, introduction to John McCallum, *That Kelly Family* (New York, 1957): xv.
7. *Ibid*.
8. Sidney Skolsky, "Let George Do It," *Times Square Tintypes* New York (1929), p. 165.
9. Corum, *op cit*.
10. Scoop Conlon, introduction to McCallum, *That Kelly Family*, p. x.
11. Montrose Moses, "George Kelly," *Theater Guild Magazine*, VII (July, 1930): 16.
12. *Ibid*.
13. Frances Wayne, Review, *Denver Times*, November 6, 1911.
14. Unidentified program note, New York Public Library Theater Collection, Lincoln Center.
15. Anon Review, *Detroit Journal*, March 30, 1914.
16. Douglas Gilbert, *American Vaudeville: Its Life and Times* (New York, 1968), pp. 113–14.
17. Anon., Review, *Dayton Star*, May 13, 1913.
18. Anon., Review, *New York Telegraph*, February 1, 1913.
19. Moses, *op. cit*.
20. Gilbert, *op. cit*., p. 156.

21. *Ibid.*, p. 15.
22. *Ibid.*, p. 205.
23. Kelly never wanted any help from his brother; he wanted to get ahead in the theater by merit rather than by "pull."
24. McCallum, *That Kelly Family*, p. 88.
25. Anon., Review, *The New York Times*, January 7, 1939.
26. McCallum, *op. cit.*, p. 87.
27. "The Virginia Judge" file, New York Public Library Theater Collection, typed manuscript, undated, unsigned.
28. Walter C. Kelly, *Of Me I Sing* (New York, 1953). Published posthumously; George Kelly worked on his brother's unfinished manuscript.
29. George Kelly, quoted in McCallum, pp. 25–26.
30. Walter Kelly, quoted in *The New York Times*, January 7, 1939.
31. Unidentified newspaper clipping, New York Public Library Theater Collection.
32. Anon., Review, *The New York Star*, November 21, 1908.
33. Gilbert, *op. cit.* p. 284.
34. Walter Kelly, *Of Me I Sing*, pp. 145–46.
35. *Ibid.*
36. *Ibid.*, p. 84.
37. Anon., "Stage News," *Variety*, January 14, 1920.
38. Anon., Interview with Kelly, *Boston Evening Transcript*, March 30, 1931.
39. Anon., Interview with Kelly, *Herald Tribune*, October 4, 1936.
40. Personal interview.
41. Anon., Interview with Kelly, *Herald Tribune*, October 4, 1936.
42. See Pauline Kael's brilliant essay "Raising Kane," *The Citizen Kane Book* (Boston, 1971), pp. 1–84, for the relationship between New York literati and the Hollywood studio system.

Chapter Two

1. Personal interview.
2. *Ibid.*
3. Carl Carmer, "George Kelly," *Theater Arts Monthly*, XV (April, 1931): 322.
4. McCarthy, *op. cit.*, p. 97.
5. Personal interview.
6. Carmer, *op. cit.*
7. Press release sent to many newspapers prior to the opening of *Maggie the Magnificent* (*Bronx Home News*, October 27, 1929).
8. Elinor Hughes, Interview, *Boston Herald*, February 27, 1945.
9. M.L.A., Interview, *Boston Sunday Globe*, March 4, 1945.
10. Stephen Rathburn, Interview, *New York Sun*, December 31, 1927.
11. Interview with Arthur Pollock, *Brooklyn Daily Eagle*, undated clipping, New York Public Library Theater Collection.

12. D.W.B., Interview, *Boston Transcript*, March 20, 1928.

13. Rathburn, *op. cit.*

14. McCarthy, *op cit.*

15. Personal interview.

16. Interview with *Herald Tribune*, February 5, 1928.

17. Personal interview.

18. Bert McCord, Interview with Kelly, *Sunday Herald Tribune*, April 29, 1945.

19. Anon., Interview with Kelly, *Herald Tribune*, February 5, 1928.

20. Edward Maisel, "The Theater of George Kelly," *Theater Arts*, XXXI (February, 1947): 39.

21. *Ibid*.

22. Arthur Wills, "The Kelly Play," *Modern Drama*, VI (December, 1963): 250. Mary McCarthy feels that the very simplicity of Kelly's moral schemes is part of the peculiar charm of his work: " . . . as in the case of the naif painter, his very faults, the crudity of his conceptions, the innocence of his allegories, become part of the subject, and, while distorting it, add to its grace." (McCarthy, *op. cit.*, p. 104.)

23. Maisel, *op. cit.*

24. *Ibid.*, p. 42.

25. *Ibid.*, p. 43.

26. Anon., Interview with Kelly, *Newsweek*, LXXV (February 2, 1970): 12.

27. Irving Drutman, *The New York Times*, December 3, 1967, Section 2, pp. 1, 3.

28. Bosley Crowther, *The New York Times*, September 27, 1936.

29. Carol Bird, Interview with George Kelly, *The Theater* XLIII (August, 1924): 24.

30. Personal interview.

31. Bird, *op. cit.*

Chapter Three

1. *Variety*, September 23, 1913.

2. *Ibid.*

3. Gilbert, *op. cit.*, p. 358.

4. *Ibid.*, p. 357.

5. *Ibid.*

6. Joseph Wood Krutch, *American Drama Since 1918* (New York, 1939), p. 61.

7. Stephen Rathburn, Interview, *New York Sun*, December 7, 1927.

8. *Ibid.*

9. Personal interview.

10. Rathburn, *op. cit.*

11. Anon., "Some Playwright Biographies," *Theater Arts*, XI (July, 1927): 12.

12. *Ibid.*
13. Personal interview.
14. Anon., "Who is George Kelly?", *The New York Times*, September 5, 1922.
15. Anon., *Cincinnati Star*, December 15, 1917.
16. Irving Drutman, Interview with Kelly, *The New York Times*, December 3, 1967.
17. Anon., "Who is George Kelly?" *op. cit.*
18. *Finders Keepers* (Cincinnati, 1922). All quotations are from this edition.
19. *The Flattering Word and Other One-Act Plays* (Boston, 1925). All quotations from the one-act plays are from this edition.
20. Anon., Review, *Boston Transcript*, April 6, 1920.
21. Personal interview. Kelly published *Finders Keepers, The Flattering Word, Poor Aubrey, The Weak Spot, Smarty's Party,* and *One of Those Things.*
22. *One of Those Things,* published in *One-Act Plays for Stage and Study, Third Series* (New York, 1927). All quotations are from this edition.
23. Krutch, *American Drama*, pp. 64–65.
24. Richard Watts, Jr., Review, *Herald Tribune*, August 18, 1927.
25. J. Brooks Atkinson, Review, *The New York Times*, August 18, 1927.
26. Anon., "A La Carte," *The Theater*, XLVI (October, 1927): 23.
27. Robert Coleman, Review, *Daily Mirror*, August 18, 1927.
28. Alison Smith, Review, *The World*, August 18, 1927.
29. *Ibid.*
30. Alan Dale, unidentified newspaper clipping, New York Public Library Theater Collection.
31. J. Brooks Atkinson, Review, *The New York Times*, August 18, 1927.
32. *Ibid.*

Chapter Four

1. Anon., Interview with Kelly, *Herald Tribune*, June 16, 1935.
2. *The Torch-Bearers* (New York, 1923). All quotations are from this edition.
3. Personal interview.
4. Heywood Broun, Review, *The World*, August 30, 1922. Many of the critics shared Broun's conviction that Kelly's wrath was incommensurate with the "crime": "He breaks an insignificant butterfly upon his funny wheel," wrote Percy Hammond in the *Herald Tribune* (August 30, 1922). This criticism—of taking seriously subjects which do not bear becoming so concerned about—was leveled at Kelly frequently throughout his career.
5. Anon., Review, *The New York Evening Post*, August 30, 1922.
6. Percy Hammond, Review, *Herald Tribune*, August 30, 1922.
7. Gilbert, *op. cit.*, p. 358.

8. Personal interview.

9. This practice of the director in permitting himself a bow was anathema to Kelly; such behavior seemed extremely unprofessional to him: "The director must not take bows. I wouldn't go out for a bow the opening night of *The Show-Off*; it would have spoiled the whole tone of the thing. I never wanted to be introduced—as director *or* author." (Personal interview.)

10. Anon., Review, *Boston Transcript*, March 20, 1923.

11. Unidentified newspaper clipping, August 30, 1922, New York Public Library Theater Collection.

12. *Ibid.*

13. Kenneth Macgowan, Review, *The Globe*, August 30, 1922.

14. Allan Downer feels Mrs. Pampinelli is a departure from the familiar types which comprise the usual Kelly dramatis personae: "Since Mrs. Pampinelli is a special type who appears infrequently on the American scene, it can only be supposed that Kelly was working off a personal grudge." (Downer, *op. cit.*, pp. 121–22.) Kelly did in fact base the character on a neighborhood woman, but there is hardly anything unrecognizable or unusual about her since she is the personification of small-town narrow-mindedness and self-satisfaction, and as such a character immediately familiar to American audiences.

15. Alexander Woollcoot, Review, *The New York Times*, August 30, 1922.

16. Robert Allerton Parker, Review, *The Independent*, December 23, 1922.

17. Carmer, *op. cit.*

18. Parker, *op. cit.*

19. Unidentified newspaper clipping, August 30, 1922, New York Public Library Theater Collection.

20. Personal interview.

21. Wills, *op. cit.*, p. 246.

22. Anon., Review, *Brooklyn Daily Eagle*, July 11, 1935.

23. Anon., Review, *Variety*, July 17, 1935. Many contemporary critics suggested the similarity between Kelly's fluttery heroine and the equally befuddled Dulcy.

24. Clive Barnes, Review, *The New York Times*, December 6, 1967.

25. Richard P. Cooke, Review, *The Wall Street Journal*, December 7, 1967.

26. Personal interview.

27. Anon., Interview with Kelly, *Herald Tribune*, March 9, 1924.

28. Drutman, *op. cit.*

29. Percy Hammond, Review, *Herald Tribune*, February 6, 1924.

30. F.L.S., Review, *Christian Science Monitor*, February 9, 1924.

31. H.F.D., Review, *Herald Tribune*, December 13, 1932.

32. Arthur Hornblow, Review, *The Theater*, XLIII (April 1924): 31.

33. John Chapman, Review, *Daily News*, December 6, 1967.

34. Downer, *op. cit.*, pp. 124–25.

35. Broun, Review, *The World*, February 6, 1924.

36. Krutch, *American Drama*, p. 62.

37. Bird, *op. cit.*

38. Alexander Woollcott, *Herald Tribune*, February 6, 1924.

39. Broun, Review, *The World*, February 6, 1924.

40. Burns Mantle, *Best Plays of 1923–1924* (New York, 1925).

41. Broun, *op. cit.*

42. Euphemia Van Rensselaer Wyatt, Review, *Catholic World*, CLXXVI (July 1950): 309.

43. Harold Clurman, Review, *The Nation*, CCVI (January 1, 1968): 27.

44. Arthur Hobson Quinn, *A History of the American Drama from the Civil War to the Present Day* (New York, 1931): II, p. 226.

45. Anon., Interview with Kelly, *Herald Tribune*, March 9, 1924.

46. Edward Sothern Hipp, Review, *Newark Evening News*, December 6, 1967.

47. Alexander Woollcott, Review, *Herald Tribune*, February 6, 1924.

48. Robert Benchley, quoted in *Current Opinion*, March 23, 1924.

49. Broun, *op. cit.*

50. McCarthy, *op. cit.*, p. 98.

51. Carmer, *op. cit.*

52. Anon., Review, *Variety*, February 7, 1924.

53. Kelly's tart, acrid domestic squabbles are neither cozy nor innocuously folksy. For example, this typically pointed exchange occurs between the play's perennial antagonists, the show-off and his mother-in-law:

Aubrey: What were you doing, handing out a line of gab about my business?

Mrs. Fisher: You haven't got any business for anybody to hand out a line of gab about—that I ever heard of.

Aubrey: Well, whether I have any business or not, it isn't necessary for you to be gabbing to perfect strangers about it. . . . What else did you tell him?

Mrs. Fisher: I told him the truth!—whatever I told him.—And I guess that's more than can be said for a whole lot *you* told him.

Aubrey: A man 'ud certainly have a swell chance trying to make anything of himself around *this hut*.

Mrs. Fisher: Listen, Boy,—any time you don't like this *hut*, you go right straight back to Lehigh Avenue to your two rooms over the dago barber shop. And I'll be glad to see your heels. . . . Nobody around here's tryin' to stop you from making' somethin' of yourself.

Aubrey: No, and nobody's trying to help me any, either; only trying to make me look like a *pin-head*—every chance they get.

Mrs. Fisher: Nobody'll have to try very hard to make *you* look like a *pin-head*; your own silly talk'll do that for you, any time at all.

54. Richard Watts, Jr., Review, *Herald Tribune*, March 17, 1934.

55. A. H. Weiler, Review, *The New York Times*, March 20, 1947.

56. Joe Pihodna, Review, *Herald Tribune*, March 20, 1947.

57. In a very helpful review, George Jean Nathan provided a stage history of the type which Harriet Craig represents:

"As far back as 1908, David Graham Phillips, though still romantic, treated one of the sex with a fair degree of realism in *The Worth of a Woman*. A year or two later, George Bronson Howard and Wilson Mizner wrote and produced *The Only Law* to show up the sentimental nonsense in the character of Laura Murdock in Eugene Walter's *The Easiest Way*. . . . Paul Armstrong then went in for an Ibsenish appraisal of his heroine in *The Escape*. And somewhere around that time Edward Knoblock tossed out an item called *Tiger! Tiger!* which startled many theatergoers with the picture of its particular hussy. The wench of Louis K. Anspacher's *The Unchastened Woman* was even more unscrupulous than Mrs. Craig, and the harridan of Martin Brown's *Cobra* more unscrupulous than both of them rolled together. . . . And in the year before Kelly's play appeared . . . O'Neill put on *Welded* and *Desire Under the Elms*, neither of whose women were precisely to be described as honeysuckles." (*The New York Journal-American*, February 17, 1947.)

58. John Mason Brown, Review, *Saturday Review*, XXX (March 8, 1947), 32–34.

59. Peggy Doyle, Review, *Boston American*, February 28, 1945.

60. Anon., Review, *The World*, October 13, 1925.

61. John Mason Brown observes that, in typically Kelly-like fashion, Mrs. Craig is an individual at the same time that she is an incarnation of a type: "Mrs. Craig is a woman with a 'humor.' Her obsession is her home, and her home is her undoing. . . . What is notable about Mr. Kelly's portrait is the way in which Mrs. Craig manages to remain an individual even while she suggests a type."

62. Anon., Interview with Kelly, *Boston Transcript*, October 25, 1926.

63. Personal interview.

64. *Ibid*.

65. *Craig's Wife* (Boston, 1926). All quotations are from this edition.

66. The reviewer for *Variety* (February 19, 1947) commented: "Despite the aura which has surrounded *Craig's Wife* as one of the minor classics of the American theater, the revival points up anew that what Kelly wrote is a perfect one-act play (the first act left to stand alone)."

67. Krutch, Review, *The Nation*, CLXIV (March 1, 1947): 256.

68. H.T.P., Review, *Boston Transcript*, April 14, 1926.

69. Gilbert W. Gabriel, Review, *The New York Sun*, October 13, 1925.

70. Personal interview.

71. George Jean Nathan, Review, *American Mercury*, VI (December, 1925): 504–05.

72. Brooks Atkinson, Review, *The New York Times*, October 13, 1925.

73. Anon., Review, *Time*, XLIX (February 24, 1947): 58.
74. Louis Kronenberger, *PM*, February 14, 1947.
75. Kappo Phelan, *Commonweal*, XLV (February 28, 1947): 492.
76. Anon., Review, *Time*, XLIX (February 24, 1947): 58.
77. D.W.B., Review, *Boston Transcript*, October 5, 1926.
78. Alan Dale, Review, *The New York American*, October 13, 1925.
79. Personal interview.
80. *Ibid*.
81. A. Hannen Swaffer, Review, *The London Times*, February 28, 1929.
82. Mordaunt Hall, Review, *The New York Times*, December 4, 1928.
83. Pressbooks in the New York Public Library Theater Collection.

Chapter Five
1. Percy Hammond, Review, *Herald Tribune*, October 26, 1926.
2. *Daisy Mayme* (Boston, 1927). All quotations are from this edition.
3. Brooks Atkinson, Review, *The New York Times*, October 26, 1926.
4. Quinn, *op. cit.*, p. 227.
5. Gilbert W. Gabriel, Review, *The New York Sun*, October 26, 1926.
6. Charles Brackett, Review, *The New Yorker*, II (November 6, 1926): 33.
7. Stark Young, Review, *The New Republic*, XLVIII (November 17, 1926): 375–76.
8. Alexander Woolcott, Review, *The World*, October 26, 1926.
9. Percy Hammond, Review, *Herald Tribune*, October 26, 1926.
10. Stark Young, *op. cit.*
11. Gilbert W. Gabriel, *The New York Sun*, October 26, 1926.
12. Brackett, *op. cit.*
13. Kelly got Roy Fant, the thirty-four-year-old actor who played the ninety-one-year-old Filoon, from vaudeville. As usual, Kelly created Filoon from "the life": his own grandfather said many of the things which Filoon says during his brief, delightful scene.
14. Personal interview.
15. Stephen Rathburn, Interview with Kelly, *The New York Sun*, December 3, 1927.
16. *Behold the Bridegroom* (Boston, 1928). All quotations are from this edition.
17. Krutch, Review, *The Nation*, CXXVI (January 11, 1928): 51.
18. Personal interview.
19. Brooks Atkinson, Review, *The New York Times*, December 27, 1927.
20. Kenneth White, "George Kelly and Dramatic Device," *Hound and Horn*, IV (April–June, 1931): 384. White feels this theme makes *Behold the Bridegroom* "a strange one among American plays." Far too generous, he writes that "the story has been, at least twice, successfully dramatized: once by Euripides in *Hippolytus*, and again by Racine in *Phèdre*." To use

Euripides and Racine as analogues to Kelly's work is altogether to mistake the Kelly tone. Kelly could no more write a tragedy in the Classic or neo-Classic mold than he could write poetic dialogue: it simply was not in Kelly's nature and to assert, as White does, that, in Kelly's hands, the Phaedra-Hippolytus theme is "more intensely tragic" than in its supposed predecessors is mere fantasy.

21. Montrose Moses in *The American Review of Reviews*, LXXVII (April 1928), p. 393, wrote: "One may see in *Behold the Bridegroom* that Kelly has not quite the full experience of knowing the class that he chooses to excoriate. Put a laundered collar on any of O'Neill's characters and he is uncomfortable in depicting them."

22. D.W.B., Review, *Boston Transcript*, March 20, 1928.

23. White, *op. cit.*

24. Stark Young, Review, *The New Republic*, LIII (January 18, 1928), p. 246, wrote: "Everyone on stage is so impressed with the seriousness of the occasion that we get to where nobody can ever make a natural elision, but must speak in the 'she cannot,' 'it does not,' 'it is very' language; and the speeches stale down into a dullish propriety like a poor translation of Ibsen. Good advice to Mr. Kelly now would be to keep his serious purpose all right enough, but to find himself gradually more at home in it."

25. Kelly is very proud of this scene. He wrote it from one in the morning until dawn; he could hardly get up from his chair at the end of it, and yet had not been conscious of the passage of time: "I had to be in it. Nothing less than great concentration was required." (Personal interview.)

26. Anon., Review, *Herald Tribune*, February 12, 1928.

27. H.T.P., Review, *Boston Transcript*, February 24, 1928.

28. Krutch, Review, *The Nation*, CXXVI (January 11, 1928): 51.

29. Interview with Samuel Spewack, *The New York Telegram*, October 23, 1929.

30. Brooks Atkinson, Interview, *The New York Times*, November 3, 1929.

31. Anonymous critic, *The Judge*, undated clipping, New York Public Library Theater Collection.

32. Arthur Pollock, *Brooklyn Daily Eagle*, October 15, 1929.

33. Krutch, Review, *The Nation*, CXXIX (November 13, 1929): 563–64.

34. Kelly felt at the time that "some of the critics dismissed the play because it dealt with a lower middle-class family which automatically stamps it 'cheap' in certain sectors of Broadway. . . . I think it is true that those who did not like the play, or at least dismissed it, did so because they felt a lower middle-class family was beneath their notice. . . . I know one manager in town who will not consider a play unless it's drawing room. This is a form of Broadway snobbery that is inexplicable to me." (Interview with Samuel Spewack, *op. cit.*)

35. *Ibid.*

36. *Ibid.*
37. Richard Dana Skinner, Review, *Commonweal*, XI (November 6, 1929): 21.
38. Stark Young, Review, *The New Republic*, LX (November 6, 1929): 325.
39. *Maggie the Magnificent*, promptbook copy in the New York Public Library Theater Collection.
40. Krutch, *op. cit.*
41. Gilbert W. Gabriel, *The New York American*, October 22, 1929.
42. Personal interview.

Chapter Six

1. Personal interview.
2. *Philip Goes Forth* (New York, 1931). All quotations are from this edition.
3. Personal interview.
4. John Mason Brown, Review, *New York Evening Post*, January 13, 1931.
5. Francis Fergusson, Review, *The Bookman*, LXXIII (March, 1931): 70.
6. Personal interview.
7. Kelly answered the criticism against La Krail by maintaining that she was drawn from life: "I was asked if I went overboard on La Krail, and I always said that the character was based on a person I knew. She always had a cape and an eccentric hat; she had just the line of talk as La Krail. She was as pale as a ghost—the Sarah Siddons of her time." (Personal interview.)
8. Euphemia van Rensselaer Wyatt, who objected to Kelly's "School of Dramatic Pedagogy," thought the ending saved the day: " . . . one forgives Mr. Kelly certain aridities for his last line when the pedagogue drops his spectacles with a wink." *Catholic World*, CXXXII (March, 1931): 722.
9. Richard Lockridge, Review, *The New York Sun*, January 13, 1931.
10. Brooks Atkinson, Review, *The New York Times*, January 13, 1931.
11. Brooks Atkinson, Review, *The New York Times*, January 18, 1931.
12. Fergusson, *op. cit.*
13. Robert Littell, Review, *The World*, January 13, 1931.
14. Wyatt, *op. cit.*
15. Brown, *op. cit.*
16. Atkinson, Review, *The New York Times*, January 18, 1931.
17. John Mason Brown, Review, *The New York Evening Post*, September 22, 1936.
18. Robert Coleman, Review, *Daily Mirror*, September 22, 1936.
19. Anon., Interview with Kelly, *The New York Times*, November 5, 1935.
20. Wolcott Gibbs, Review, *The New Yorker*, XII (October 3, 1936): 30.

21. Anon., Review, *The Literary Digest*, CXXII (October 3, 1936): 19.
22. Joseph Wood Krutch, *The Nation*, CXLII (October 3, 1936): 401.
23. *Reflected Glory* (New York, 1937). All quotations are from this edition.
24. Hanlon's perfectionism is clearly an echo of Kelly's own methods—but in every other respect the character is foreign to Kelly's temperament. In her autobiography (*Tallulah*, [New York, 1952], p. 220), Miss Bankhead wrote: "[Kelly's] singularly free of the brashness and vulgarity which often sullies even the ablest people in the theater. His attitude toward life is Olympian. . . . Both he and Thornton Wilder have a cloistered air that sets them apart from the playwrights with whom I've had traffic. Never have I seen Kelly waver in his professional code. He is a gentleman!" The same certainly cannot be said for the gruff, high-strung Hanlon.
25. Anon., Interview with Kelly, *Herald Tribune*, October 4, 1936.
26. Stark Young, Review, *The New Republic*, LXXXVIII (October 7, 1936): 257.
27. Gilbert W. Gabriel, Review, *The New York American*, September 22, 1936.
28. *Ibid*.

Chapter Seven

1. Personal interview.
2. Louis Kronenberger, Review, *PM*, March 20, 1945.
3. John Chapman, Review, *Daily News*, March 20, 1945.
4. Personal interview.
5. Kronenberger, Review, *PM*, April 7, 1945.
6. *The Deep Mrs. Sykes* (New York, 1946). All quotations are from this edition.
7. Lewis Nichols, Review, *The New York Times*, March 20, 1945.
8. Arthur Pollock, Review, *Brooklyn Daily Eagle*, March 20, 1945.
9. Irene Kittle, Review, *Cue*, March 24, 1945.
10. Kappo Phelan, Review, *Commonweal*, XLI (April 6, 1945): 625.
11. Joseph Wood Krutch, Review, *The Nation*, CLX (April 7, 1945): 395.
12. Rosamund Gilder, Review, *Theater Arts*, XXIX (May, 1945): 271.
13. Personal interview.
14. Theater Guild press release, November, 1946, in file of The Theater Collection of The New York Public Library at Lincoln Center.
15. Mary McCarthy, *op. cit.*, p. 103.
16. Krutch, Review, *The Nation*, CLXIV (March 1, 1947): 256.
17. Some of the reviewers were unhappy about Kelly's unorthodox ending. Brooks Atkinson, for instance, found Kelly's "final solutions . . . positively gruesome—the middle-aged philanderer marrying his mistress . . . the divorced mother sneaking off like a demented matron to her former husband's wedding." (*The New York Times*, November 20, 1946.)

18. *The Fatal Weakness* (New York, 1947). All quotations are from this edition.

19. Krutch, *op. cit.*

20. *Ibid.*

21. Kappo Phelan, Review, *Commonweal*, XLV (December 6, 1946): 201.

22. Anon., Review, *Variety* (October 23, 1946).

23. Wolcott Gibbs, Review, *The New Yorker*, XXII (November 30, 1946); 60.

24. Jack Kroll, Review, *Newsweek*, LXXII (December 18, 1967): 76.

Selected Bibliography

PRIMARY SOURCES

Behold the Bridegroom. Boston: Little, Brown, 1928.
Craig's Wife. Boston: Little, Brown, 1926.
Daisy Mayme. Boston: Little, Brown, 1927.
The Deep Mrs. Sykes. New York: Samuel French, 1946.
The Fatal Weakness. New York: Samuel French, 1947.
Finders Keepers. Cincinnati: Stewart Kidd Co., 1923.
The Flattering and Other One-Act Plays. Boston: Little, Brown, 1925.
Maggie the Magnificent. Promptbook copy in the Theater Collection of the New York Public Library.
One of Those Things, published in *One-Act Plays for Stage and Study, Third Series*. New York: Samuel French, 1927.
Philip Goes Forth. New York: Samuel French, 1931.
Reflected Glory. New York: Samuel French, 1937.
The Show-Off. Boston: Little, Brown, 1924.
The Torch-Bearers. New York: American Library Service, 1923.

SECONDARY SOURCES

1. Books

To date no full-length studies of George Kelly have been published. The standard surveys of American drama give Kelly scant attention; the Kelly bibliography consists, therefore, of newspaper and magazine reviews listed in Notes and References. The following books, however, do contain material on Kelly not readily available elsewhere.

BANKHEAD, TALLULAH. *Tallulah: My Autobiography*. New York: Harper & Bros., 1952. Contains anecdotes that suggest Kelly's thoroughly professional and gentlemanly code.
DOWNER, ALAN S. *Fifty Years of American Drama. 1900–1950*. Chicago: Henry Regnery Co., 1951. Kelly gets brief mention as an early American Realist, one of a group of playwrights of the 1920's who took American drama out of its Dark Ages.

GILBERT, DOUGLAS. *American Vaudeville. Its Life and Times*. New York: Dover, 1968. Vivid account of the history and the flavor of vaudeville; Kelly is mentioned only briefly as a "high-class" sketch writer, but the book provides a detailed background for the kind of theater in which Kelly received his early training.

KELLY, WALTER C. *Of Me I Sing. An Informal Autobiography*. New York: The Dial Press, 1953. Life and times of Kelly's jaunty older brother, the famed vaudeville monologuist. Also gives colorful views of vaudeville, Hollywood, and the Kelly family; George gets affectionate mention now and then.

KRUTCH, JOSEPH WOOD. *The American Drama Since 1918*. New York: Random House, 1939. Standard work in the field; Krutch, one of the most sensitive and responsive critics in regard to Kelly's work, is much better on Kelly in his splendid reviews for *The Nation*; here, he merely offers a general overview of a favorite playwright.

McCALLUM, JOHN. *That Kelly Family*. New York: A. S. Barnes & Co., 1957. Provides biographical material not easily available. Concentrates on the sports figures of the Kelly family; rather absurdly right-wing in its approach, but something of the Kelly personality is included here.

MANTLE, BURNS. *Contemporary American Playwrights*. New York: Dodd, Mead & Co., 1939. Brief, but helpful, biographical sketch; some comments from Kelly on dramatic method.

MOSES, MONTROSE J. *The American Dramatist*. Boston: Little, Brown, 1925. An early assessment by one of Kelly's most enthusiastic admirers.

2. Articles

The number of serious articles devoted to Kelly is quite small; again, the reader is referred to the newspaper and magazine reviews listed in Notes and References. However, the reviews in *The Nation* by Joseph Wood Krutch and those in *The New Republic* by Stark Young are especially recommended.

CARMER, CARL. "George Kelly." *Theater Arts Monthly*, XV (April 1931): 322–30. Excellent assessment of Kelly's achievement up to and including *Philip Goes Forth*. Examines the impact of Kelly's vaudeville experiences; regrets that the Kelly Play has become too much of a familiar commodity; asks for a change in method but wants Kelly to emphasize his comic rather than his sober side.

CROWDER, FLORENCE. "Up from Vaudeville to the Front Rank of American Dramatists." *Letters*, V (February 1932): 29–33. Remarkably foolish article, misinformed, and a pastiche of newspaper quotations. Claims that Kelly will probably never be able to get above "regulation shop-made plays."

McCARTHY, MARY. "George Kelly." *Mary McCarthy's Theater Chronicles 1937–1962*. New York: Farrar, Straus & Co., 1963. The single most incisive comment ever written on Kelly. Captures exactly the flavor, the spirit, the peculiarities, of the Kelly Play.

MAISEL, EDWARD. "The Theater of George Kelly." *Theater Arts*, XXXI (February 1947): 39–43. Stresses Kelly's theme of vocation—finding the right job and doing it professionally. Links the vocation theme to Kelly's Puritan outlook.

MOSES, MONTROSE J. "George Kelly." *Theater Guild Magazine*, VII (July 1930): 15–17. Overdoes Kelly's moralistic fervor, his Puritan ethic, and his religious background.

VAN DRUTEN, JOHN. "Small Souls and Great Plays." *Theater Arts Monthly*, XI (July 1927): 493–98. Appreciation of Kelly's meticulously detailed method, his severely restricted focus, his "small" people and his large plays.

WHITE, KENNETH. "George Kelly and Dramatic Device." *Hound and Horn*, IV (April–June 1931): 384–400. Concentrates on *Behold the Bridegroom* as a classic American tragedy.

WILLS, ARTHUR. "The Kelly Play." *Modern Drama*, VI (December 1963): 245–55. Sensible overview. Reviews the Kelly themes, considers the qualities that give the Kelly Play individual distinction, discusses Kelly's similarities to, and departures from, American Realism.

3. Bibliography

DOYLE, PAUL. "George Kelly: An Eclectic Bibliography." *Bulletin of Bibliography*, XXIV (September–December 1965): 173–74, 177. Thorough bibliography of primary and secondary sources; includes list of significant reviews of individual plays and one of Kelly's unproduced and unpublished plays.

Index

Albee, Edward: *Tiny Alice*, 33
Anderson, Judith, 31
Anderson, Maxwell, 25
Armstrong, Paul: *Woman Proposes*, 19,
  35, 37
Arzner, Dorothy, 74
Atkinson, Brooks, 79, 89, 99

Bankhead, Tallulah, 31, 74, 101, 102
Barnes, Clive, 59
Barry, Philip, 25, 26, 119
Bartels, John Louis, 30
Baxter, Warner, 74
Beery, Wallace, 23
Behrman, S. N., 25, 26, 119
Belasco, David, 52
Benchley, Robert, 63
Blondell, Joan, 31, 94
Brackett, Charles, 79, 81
Brooklyn Eagle, 89
Broun, Heywood, 52, 60
Brown, John Mason, 100
Burke, Billie, 58

Cagney, James, 31, 94
Carmer, Carl, 26, 55
Chapman, John, 107
Chekhov, Anton, 80, 81, 119
Civic Repertory Theater, 25, 75
Claire, Ina, 107, 117
Common Law, The, 17, 18, 35
Commonweal, 91
Conlon, Scoop, 16
Crawford, Joan, 74

Doubting Thomas, 58

Evelyn, Judith, 73

Federal Theater, 67
Ferguson, Francis, 97
Fitch, Clyde: *Girl With Green Eyes*, 24

Gabriel, Gilbert W., 79, 80
Gibbs, Wolcott, 102
Gilbert, Douglas, 19, 21, 36
Gildea, Mary, 30
Gilder, Rosamund, 113

Hammond, Percy, 52, 80
Harriet Craig, 74
Hayes, Helen, 67
Herald Tribune (N.Y.), 67
Herne, Chrystal, 29, 31, 73
Howard, Sidney, 25, 119; *The Silver
  Cord*, 26
Hull, Josephine, 31

Ibsen, Henrik, 24, 80, 81, 119

James, Henry, 108
Jones, Henry Arthur, 73, 84, 113
Judge, 89

Kaufman, George S., 25; *Stage Door*,
  106; *The Royal Family*, 106
Kelly, George: as actor, 17–19; dialogue,
  examples of, 46, 61, 64–65, 81–82, 92,
  104, 110–111, 117; as director, 28–29;
  in Hollywood, 22–23, 107; influences
  on, 17; instinctive playwright, 24–26;
  moralist, 31; place in American theater, 118–120; plays about theater,

95–106; plays as films, 67, 74; plays, basic substance of, 26–27; plays, popular, 50–74; plays, production of, 27–31; puritanism, 88; relationship with actors, 30–31; rules for dramatic technique, 35–36; social philosophy, 21, 22; theater business, 13; vaudeville sketches, 35–49

WORKS:
A La Carte, 47–49
Behold the Bridegroom, 31, 32, 75, 83–88, 89
Between Numbers, 48
Can Two Walk Together?, 32, 107
Craig's Wife, 7, 24, 26, 31, 39, 44, 50, 68–74, 78, 80, 90, 91, 107, 108
Daisy Mayme, 31, 32, 33, 36, 46, 48, 50, 75–83, 90
Deep Mrs. Sykes, The, 32, 36, 39, 45, 95, 107, 108, 109–114, 115
Fatal Weakness, The, 32, 36, 39, 95, 107, 108, 114–118
Finders Keepers, 17, 18, 32, 33, 36, 37–40
Flattering Word, The, 18, 32, 40–41, 105
Hotel Porch, The, 48
Maggie the Magnificent, 25, 31, 33, 36, 50, 75, 88–94
Mrs. Ritter Appears, 36
Old Hutch, 23
One of Those Things, 36, 41–43
Philip Goes Forth, 26, 32, 33, 41, 51, 95, 96–101, 105, 112
Poor Aubrey, 36, 65, 66
Reflected Glory, 31, 48, 51, 95, 101–106, 107
Show-Off, The, 7, 27, 29, 30, 33, 36, 46, 50, 58–68, 72, 73, 74, 78, 79, 86, 90, 91, 112, 118
Smarty's Party, 32, 33, 36, 42, 43–45
Torch-Bearers, The, 7, 13, 32, 36, 41, 48, 49, 50, 51–58, 59, 60, 61, 62, 65, 66, 67, 72, 74, 97, 105, 108
Weak Spot, The, 42, 45–47, 108
When All Else Fails, 107

Kelly, Grace, 16
Kelly, Gregory, 67
Kelly, John, 16
Kelly, Walter, 16, 19–22; *Of Me I Sing*, 21
Kroll, Jack, 118
Kronenberger, Louis, 109, 118
Krutch, Joseph Wood, 36, 44, 61, 71, 88, 90, 93, 102, 113, 115, 117, 118
Kummer, Clare: *Rollo's Wild Oats*, 56

LaShelle, Kirk: *The Virginian*, 17, 18, 35
Le Gallienne, Eva, 25, 75
London, England, 73
Lowell, Helen, 29

McCallum, John, 16
McCarthy, Mary, 7, 30, 40, 65, 115, 118
Macgowan, Kenneth, 55, 57
Maisel, Edward, 32
Metro-Goldwyn-Mayer, 67
Miller, Arthur: *Death of a Salesman*, 63
Moses, Montrose, 17

New York Evening Post, 52
New York Times, 38, 59, 67, 79, 89, 99
New Yorker, 79
Newsweek, 118

O'Neill, Eugene, 25, 64, 118

Pantomime Rehearsal, A, 55
Pastor, Tony, 19
Phelan, Kappo, 113, 117
Pinero, Arthur Wing, 73, 84, 113
Pollock, Arthur, 89
Provincetown Playhouse, 25
Pulitzer Prize, 68

Quinn, Arthur Hobson, 79

Redding, Francesca: *A Happy Pair*, 19
Rice, Elmer, 25
Rich, Irene, 74
Rogers, Will, 20, 58
Russell, Rosalind, 74

Saturday Evening Post, 23

Scribe, Eugene, 13
Skelton, Red, 67
Skinner, Richard Dana, 91
Skipworth, Alison, 58
Stewart, Rosalie, 30, 47
Strindberg, August, 24
Sturges, Preston, 25

Theater Guild, 25
Tracy, Lee, 29
Tracy, Spencer, 67

Variety, 35, 58
Vokes, Rosina, 55, 56

Watts, Richard, 67
Weiler, A. H., 67
Willard, Catherine, 29
Wister, Owen: *The Virginian,* 17, 18, 35
Woollcott, Alexander, 55, 63, 80
World, The (N.Y.), 63

Young, Stark, 91, 118